VOL 37 / PART 2
May–August 2021

Edited by **Helen Paynter** and **David Spriggs**

7   **Hebrews**
    Rosalee Velloso Ewell   *3–23 May*

29 **Ezra**
    Pauline Hoggarth   *24–30 May*

37 **Mark 11—13**
    Steve Motyer   *31 May–20 June*

59 **Revelation 1—11: drawing back the curtain**
    Stephen Finamore   *21 June–4 July*

72 **Isaiah 56—66**
    C.L. Crouch   *5–25 July*

95 **Honour and shame**
    Philip Grasham   *26 July–1 August*

103 **1 Corinthians**
    Nigel G. Wright   *2–22 August*

126 **2 Kings 1—13**
    Alison Lo   *23 August–5 September*

The Bible Reading Fellowship
15 The Chambers, Vineyard
Abingdon OX14 3FE
brf.org.uk

The Bible Reading Fellowship (BRF) is a Registered Charity (233280)

ISBN 978 1 80039 035 5
All rights reserved

This edition © The Bible Reading Fellowship 2021
Cover image © Alena/stock.adobe.com

Distributed in Australia by:
MediaCom Education Inc, PO Box 610, Unley, SA 5061
Tel: 1 800 811 311 | admin@mediacom.org.au

Distributed in New Zealand by:
Scripture Union Wholesale, PO Box 760, Wellington
Tel: 04 385 0421 | suwholesale@clear.net.nz

Acknowledgements
Scripture quotations marked with the following acronyms are taken from the
version shown. Where no acronym is given, the quotation is taken from the version
stated in the contributor's introduction. NRSV: The New Revised Standard Version
of the Bible, Anglicised edition, copyright © 1989, 1995 by the Division of Christian
Education of the National Council of the Churches of Christ in the United States
of America. Used by permission. All rights reserved. CEB: Copyright © 2011 by
Common English Bible. NIV: The Holy Bible, New International Version (Anglicised
edition) copyright © 1979, 1984, 2011 by Biblica. Used by permission of Hodder
& Stoughton Publishers, a Hachette UK company. All rights reserved. 'NIV' is a
registered trademark of Biblica. UK trademark number 1448790. ESV: The Holy
Bible, English Standard Version, published by HarperCollins Publishers, © 2001
Crossway Bibles, a division of Good News Publishers. Used by permission. All
rights reserved.

Every effort has been made to trace and contact copyright owners for material used
in this resource. We apologise for any inadvertent omissions or errors, and would
ask those concerned to contact us so that full acknowledgement can be made in
the future.

A catalogue record for this book is available from the British Library

Printed by Gutenberg Press, Tarxien, Malta

Suggestions for using *Guidelines*

Set aside a regular time and place, if possible, when and where you can read and pray undisturbed. Before you begin, take time to be still and, if you find it helpful, use the BRF Prayer on page 6.

In *Guidelines*, the introductory section provides context for the passages or themes to be studied, while the units of comment can be used daily, weekly or whatever best fits your timetable. You will need a Bible (more than one if you want to compare different translations) as Bible passages are not included. Please don't be tempted to skip the Bible reading because you know the passage well. We will have utterly failed if we don't bring our readers into engagement with the word of God. At the end of each week is a 'Guidelines' section, offering further thoughts about or practical application of what you have been studying.

Occasionally, you may read something in *Guidelines* that you find particularly challenging, even uncomfortable. This is inevitable in a series of notes which draws on a wide spectrum of contributors and doesn't believe in ducking difficult issues. Indeed, we believe that *Guidelines* readers much prefer thought-provoking material to a bland diet that only confirms what they already think.

If you do disagree with a contributor, you may find it helpful to go through these three steps. First, think about why you feel uncomfortable. Perhaps this is an idea that is new to you, or you are not happy about the way something has been expressed. Or there may be something more substantial – you may feel that the writer is guilty of sweeping generalisation, factual error, or theological or ethical misjudgement. Second, pray that God would use this disagreement to teach you more about his word and about yourself. Third, have a deeper read about the issue. There are further reading suggestions at the end of each writer's block of notes. And then, do feel free to write to the contributor or the editor of *Guidelines*. We welcome communication, by email, phone or letter, as it enables us to discover what has been useful, challenging or infuriating for our readers. We don't always promise to change things, but we will always listen and think about your ideas, complaints or suggestions. Thank you!

To send feedback, please email **enquiries@brf.org.uk**, phone **+44 (0)1865 319700** or write to the address shown opposite.

Writers in this issue

Rosalee Velloso Ewell is a theologian from São Paulo, Brazil. She is director of church relations for the United Bible Societies and former principal of Redcliffe College. Rosalee lives with her family in Birmingham, UK.

Pauline Hoggarth was born in Peru. She taught modern languages in Scotland and London before serving with Scripture Union in three different roles in the UK and overseas. She is the author of *The Seed and the Soil: Engaging with the word of God* (Langham, 2011) and in retirement enjoys occasional opportunities to help people to think creatively about the Bible, most recently in Korea.

Steve Motyer taught New Testament at London School of Theology and led the Theology and Counselling programme there before retiring in 2016. He is the author of a few books on the Bible and related themes, most notably on the second coming of Jesus. He is a proud father and grandfather and helps to lead his church in Watford.

Stephen Finamore is principal of Bristol Baptist College. He is married to Rebecca and their two daughters are Debbie and Jen. Steve has worked as a pastor, a lawyer and in community development in inner London and the Peruvian Andes.

C.L. Crouch is David Allan Hubbard Professor of Old Testament at Fuller Theological Seminary in Pasadena, California and author of several books, including *An Introduction to the Study of Jeremiah* and *Isaiah: An introduction and study guide*.

Philip Grasham is a part-time lecturer for Moorlands College. Previously, he worked for eight years with BMS World Mission as a mission trainer and twelve years with WEC International in various roles in the UK and west Africa.

Nigel G. Wright is principal emeritus of Spurgeon's College. He is also a former president of the Baptist Union of Great Britain. Born in Manchester, he was ordained to ministry in 1973 and has served in two growing churches in the north-west of England. He is married to Judy. They have two children and three grandchildren and live in Winsford, Cheshire.

Alison Lo is associate professor of Old Testament at Bethel Seminary, Minnesota. Previously she taught at the Chinese University of Hong Kong, London School of Theology, Moorlands Midlands Centre in the UK and Baptist Theological Seminary, Singapore.

Helen Paynter writes...

Because of the necessarily long lead times that publishers work with, I am writing this editor's introduction in May 2020. We are at the height (?) of the biggest peacetime crisis that our country has known for generations. Tens of thousands have died, we have all faced the possibility of our own mortality and we have all experienced enormous restrictions to our normal freedoms.

What this means, in terms of *Guidelines*, is that most of the contributions in this issue have been written under these intensely difficult circumstances. Contributors have been facing their own domestic concerns. Those who are pastors have been trying to work out how to look after their churches in these rapidly changing times. The theological educators have been finding new ways of delivering material, assessing students and ensuring that academic standards are maintained. All of our contributors will have experienced difficulty in accessing books and resources that they might normally have consulted.

I say none of this as an apology for what this issue contains – I don't believe that any apology is needed – but as a testimony to the tenacity and brilliance of my colleagues. In the middle of unexpected busyness, they have managed to meet publication deadlines. In the midst of anxiety, they have written with faith and hope. During times of testing, they have proved faithful. I am grateful to God for each one of them.

So, what do we have to offer you this time? We have familiar and well-loved faces. Steve Motyer continues his much-appreciated tour of Mark's gospel. C.L. Crouch, who has previously written for us on Hosea, makes a welcome return with some helpful notes on what might be termed 'Trito-Isaiah'. Nigel Wright returns with an excellent three-week series on 1 Corinthians. And Pauline Hoggarth gives us a thought-provoking week on Ezra.

I'm also delighted to introduce some new writers to you. Alison Lo is associate professor of Old Testament at Bethel Seminary, Minnesota, and she will take you through the first part of 2 Kings – that weird world where animals do the bidding of humans, and horses and chariots of fire keep showing up. Phil Grasham, writing out of years of cross-cultural missionary experience, helps us to see how an appreciation for honour and shame enhances our reading of the biblical text. Rosalee Velloso Ewell, former principal of Redcliffe College, Gloucester, gives us a scintillating tour of Hebrews. And finally, we have something rather original to offer. Stephen Finamore is an expert on the book of Revelation, and takes an imaginative approach to help us to find our way into it more deeply than usual.

I think this is an exciting edition of *Guidelines*, forged in 'interesting times'. May it bless you as you use it.

The BRF Prayer

Almighty God,
you have taught us that your word is a lamp for our feet
and a light for our path. Help us, and all who prayerfully
read your word, to deepen our fellowship with you
and with each other through your love.
And in so doing may we come to know you more fully,
love you more truly, and follow more faithfully
in the steps of your son Jesus Christ, who lives and reigns
with you and the Holy Spirit, one God forevermore.
Amen

Hebrews

Rosalee Velloso Ewell

An unknown author, a secret audience, coded signs, dangerous times, supernatural creatures: Hebrews has all the ingredients for a thrilling novel. But far from fictional, Hebrews speaks to a very real and new world made possible by the death and resurrection of Jesus. Without using academic Christological terms, it presents us with all the strangeness, wonder, humanity and divinity of Jesus.

Hebrews is unique in the ways it challenges its readers, then and now, to grasp and enter this new world shaped by the cross and resurrection. The new world is at odds with the powers of this world and with most things 21st-century Christians might call 'normal'. The Christ-shaped life to which we are called demands nothing less than suffering, enduring persecution and an uncompromising character that witnesses to God's kingdom and rejoices in the victory of Christ.

Though we know it through words on a page, Hebrews might have been written as a sermon or persuasive speech. Therefore, these guidelines refer both to 'listeners' and 'readers' so as to keep this point in mind. Despite all attempts at historical reconstruction and analysis of the content and context of Hebrews, one can only speculate about authorship, first audience, location and date of its composition. The unknown author was likely skilled in rhetoric and knew how to send coded messages to his readers, aware of the dangers that they all faced as Christians in the Roman empire. One clue to this is the use of the Greek letter 'tau', which translates as our 't'. As the author makes the case for the supremacy of Christ, there is this veiled allusion through sign and sound to the horror of the cross as the means by which Jesus was exalted.

The historical puzzles and rhetoric are not what make Hebrews a demanding book to read. Rather, it is 'the way Hebrews challenges our construction of the world, our image of Jesus, and our understanding of discipleship that makes reading it truly difficult' (Johnson, p. 2). Hebrews signposts a way of life in God's new reality through the suffering and death of Christ. To those signs we now turn.

Unless otherwise stated, Bible quotations are from the NRSV. Author references are to works in the 'Further reading' list.

1 In the beginning... was the end

Hebrews 1:1–4

Right at the start, Hebrews calls to mind the God of all creation. God does not need his creation, but he chose to engage with it, to love it and to speak to it from the very beginning. Fast-forward to the climax and end of this story – the Son who was there from the start and who is the subject of all that is to follow in this letter.

These introductory verses are not typical of other letters in the New Testament. They don't tell us who the author is, to whom he/she is writing (note that in these notes I use 'he' for ease); it doesn't even begin with praising God or a prayer for the hearers' well-being. Without mincing words, the author gets right to the heart of the argument of the entire epistle and begins with the end – 'but in these last days' (v. 2) – and then draws the listener into the arguments that demonstrate this reality of which God has spoken all along. The framework of the argument is the constant contrast of the continuity and discontinuity of God's communication with humanity (Johnson, p. 64).

The author's audience is suffering persecution. He needs to persuade them not to give up. In order to do so, he sets out the story of the superiority of the Son, the only one worthy of allegiance and devotion. In fact, part and parcel of discipleship is the suffering that comes from such discipleship. This path of discipleship and worship is only possible because Christ himself was both suffering servant and the one exalted to the right hand of the Father.

God is active within scripture and within the fabric of the universe. These initial verses in Hebrews follow patterns of Judaic literature which show the many ways God's creative power and glory are reflected in the world. But the author of Hebrews goes beyond this – Jesus is not just a sign or a mirror. Rather, he is the exact imprint of God. The Greek term used here for 'imprint' is our English word for 'character'. Latin American theologian C. René Padilla once said, 'In Christ God contextualised himself.' Hebrews is telling us just this and inviting us to keep our eyes fixed ever on this Jesus, who is God himself.

2 Do not overestimate the importance of angels

Hebrews 1:5–14

The early Christians and all the writers of the New Testament, most of whom were Jews, assumed that Jesus was the Messiah spoken of in the Hebrew scriptures. The writer of Hebrews is no exception, and he quotes in this passage Psalm 2, which was one of the Old Testament passages most often used by early Christians to refer to Jesus. It is worth noting that the name 'Jesus' is kept in suspense until 2:9.

When a community is under pressure, it is sometimes easier for it to go back to what is familiar or more socially acceptable than to endure conflict and persecution. Life was hard for Jewish Christians. They were threatened by civil and religious authorities, and many were outcasts of their own families. The author of Hebrews knew the power that tradition and legalism have over people, especially when they seek a way out of trouble. In order to keep his listeners' eyes fixed on Jesus and to invite them into a fuller life of discipleship, he builds his argument for why Jesus is superior to anything his listeners might be tempted to return to, especially their old traditions. Drawing on scripture, Hebrews shows that from the very beginning God intended the Son to be higher than the angels. The gospel that these people first heard was indeed a fulfilment of all that had come before. It is almost as if the author says to his hearers, 'Remember your first love and the reasons you loved. Those are still the most important reasons, so persevere in this love.'

Angels and archangels are mere messengers used by God to bring humans into relationship with God. They are important creatures who serve a fundamental purpose in God's plans. However, that purpose has been accomplished in the coming of God's Son. Angels are created beings who worship God's Son, so why would one worship angels?

A community under threat wants justice. It also desires peace and prosperity. Hebrews reminds its audience that such justice, peace and prosperity have only one true origin and only one who can guarantee that to them. Even under persecution, we are promised that only in Christ is God's justice and peace fulfilled (vv. 8–9). Therefore, listeners are urged to persevere. Salvation is their ultimate reward.

3 We see through a glass dimly... but we do see Jesus

Hebrews 2:1–9

There is a very pastoral and caring tone to this passage as the author reminds the suffering people that they are indeed the heirs of salvation mentioned in the previous section (1:14). They have heard a message that demands a response. This is not the type of hearing that is passive. Rather, it is a message that prompts one either to follow and move forward or to fail.

The penalties for disobedience will be dealt with later in the letter. For now, the focus is on the security believers have in God's word. It is a twofold security: first, it is a word firmly established by the Lord himself and witnessed by others (v. 4); second, God has sent the Holy Spirit to enable the right response to it. God does not demand obedience without also providing his people with the means and gifts to enable them to obey.

Obedience has its perfect result not simply in the rescuing of humanity from sin, but in making it possible for us to enter the 'coming world', that is, Christ's glory (v. 5). The author quotes from Psalm 8:4–6 to argue this point even more strongly. All of what God has done through Jesus has been for us, for humanity, not for the angels. Everything is at stake in our response, including participation in the new reality inaugurated by Jesus.

Scholars have noted the similarities between some themes in Hebrews and Paul's first letter to the Corinthians. The second part of verse 8 is one such echo. This is a pilgrim's journey that must go through suffering and death. The path to salvation and the guide are one and the same: Jesus in all his affliction and death, and in his exaltation and glory.

In the course of history, Christians have often struggled to understand how Jesus can be fully human and fully divine. The argument in Hebrews for the two natures of Christ appears in a nutshell in verse 9. We do not first understand what it means to be human and then try to see how Jesus fits or not in our definitions. Instead, only in Christ do we know what true humanity is and is intended to be. Jesus, the truly obedient one, is humanity's representative and as such is ruler of all creation, past, present and future.

4 For the salvation of Moses and his siblings

In traditional Judaism the mark of the people of God was their obedience to the law of Moses. This law was handed to Moses by the angels sent from God. The author of Hebrews is eager to prove to his listeners that Jesus has not come to overthrow the law or the promises made to Abraham and his children, but that Jesus is actually the one true child. Jesus is the one through whom God fulfils all those promises.

One of the big distinctions between Christianity and Islam is that through Jesus, Christians are able to call God 'Father'. This passage in Hebrews explains more than any other what is at stake in understanding Jesus as the firstborn of God's family and as our brother. There are three ways the author of Hebrews elaborates this point: first, Jesus is the pioneer of salvation (2:10), who goes where no one else has gone before – to die – and comes out victorious; second, it is the particularity of Christ's suffering and death that frees us from the fear of death (2:14–15); and third, Jesus is the high priest who offers himself as a sacrifice on our behalf (2:17). Out of pure love, as our older brother, Christ – the truly human one – enters the reality of the suffering and death of God's creation, but he overcomes these and so prepares the way for us to follow.

A friend once told me, 'The problem with humans is that we fear death more than we fear God.' This was also the case for those who received this letter. Fear can turn people inwards and make them forget their purpose and mission. The disciples were afraid for their lives as they huddled in the upper room after Jesus' crucifixion (John 20:19). It took the risen Christ's presence to break through their fears and show them God's glory. Hebrews addresses this fear by reminding us that Jesus entered into our fear of suffering and death more fully than anyone else and overcame that death by God's own power. Therefore, we are saved from such fear and empowered to follow our older brother with confidence and hope (3:6).

Finally, the author introduces a theme that will be developed more fully later in the story. Jesus is not only the heir and firstborn (1:2, 6), pioneer (2:10), sanctifier (2:11), apostle (3:1) and builder (3:3), but he is also the merciful and faithful high priest (2:17; 3:1) who also embodies the sacrifice. Among the canon, only Hebrews portrays Jesus as the priest who is also of royal lineage. In so doing, Hebrews offers us an image of Christ that is so multifaceted and amazing that it cannot be easily categorised in our simple human terms.

5 Remembering Psalm 95

Within the greater narrative of Hebrews, there is an echo of Psalm 95 and the grand story of Israel as God's chosen people. 'In the beginning God spoke' recalls Moses and the giving of the law. In this section, we wander the wilderness with the Israelites. Later, Hebrews will recall this time of testing and the demands that come on those who obey. Finally, there is the victory of God. Hebrews invites its readers into this story, reminding them they were already a part of it from the beginning, but now the time has come to learn from the mistakes of the past.

In many Christian churches, morning prayers often begin with Psalm 95. It is a psalm that has always intrigued me because of the sharp change in tone from verses 7 to 8 and because of the dramatic last phrase, 'They shall not enter my rest' (Psalm 95:11). The writer to the Hebrews refers to this psalm frequently and plays with time as the argument builds. In Hebrews 3:16–18 the psalm belongs to those who followed Moses out of Egypt and wandered the desert, vacillating between obedience and disobedience to God's commandments, until finally their rebellion kept them from entering the promised land. In verses 7, 13 and 15 the author places the psalm firmly in the context of his listeners and their struggles under persecution. Today, this is about you! Psalm 95 also serves the larger, grander story of all God's dealings with his people. Unbelief is always a temptation and danger for the people of God.

Sin is deceptive (v. 13) and is much like a blind spot. By definition we cannot see it, and therefore we rely on others to point out such areas of blindness. 'Caution! Unbelief ahead!' is what the author of Hebrews is saying here. Like the Israelites in the desert, these people are wandering and unsure of their future. That fear is at the root of unbelief and rebellion and can lead them to take their eyes off Jesus and to try to take matters into their own hands. Fear undermines the confidence that one had upon first encountering Christ. Sin and fear are also systemic and can infiltrate a community, leading to its devastation. Therefore, the author warns, we need one another. We do not follow Christ alone. Rather, our pilgrimage of obedient discipleship and our future in God require that we participate in a community that holds one another up and that keeps the other from developing a hardened heart.

6 Restful obedience

The danger of unbelief is also the danger of losing one's identity. The quality of the Christian character described in Hebrews, which is the character to which all are called, is decisively counter to what the recipients of this letter were hearing in their context. It is also qualitatively different to our present-day contexts. Hebrews demands very much of those who claim to follow Christ.

Yet despite the high demands on God's people, Hebrews also shows how God has provided a way, through Christ and the Spirit, for his people to enter the future promise, already inaugurated by Jesus. Entering into God's rest is not only a live option for humanity; it is the only option if we are to maintain that identity that we were given in Christ. Here, again, there is the image of unity in the community – we need one another; we need to be united by faith (v. 2) in order to be fully obedient.

Again the author of Hebrews plays with time. There are three 'rests' in this passage: God's rest after creation (v. 4); the 'rest' for those who entered the promised land with Joshua after the 40 years of wilderness wanderings (v. 8); and the 'rest' that is in the Psalm 95 quotation (v. 5). Whether David or someone else wrote the psalm, it was clearly composed long after Joshua and the people entered the land. Thus Hebrews concludes, the psalm must be pointing to another rest, a future rest (Wright, pp. 36–37). As with the entire argument of the book, that future rest is God's gift. It is God's future, which is made possible for all who believe in Jesus. As Wright points out, there is a play on the names of Joshua and Jesus, which in Hebrew and Greek are the same. Joshua lead the people into their first rest, but Jesus leads them into the final and future rest.

Even in rest, God's word is active, exposing both the belief and unbelief of God's people. Everyone is subject to this scrutiny. Therefore, the writer urges his listeners to practise that faith today, before unbelief sets in. The people must not take their eyes off Jesus, for only through faith will they enter God's rest.

Guidelines

- The world imagined by Hebrews is one constructed by scripture (Johnson, p. 45). Scripture shapes the letter's argument for the centrality of Christ, but also points to God and to God's Son and to the new reality inaugurated in Jesus' suffering, death and resurrection. It is this new world, God's future, that is 'really real'. Unlike those who first received this letter, Christians today are not shaped by biblical symbolism, nor do most see their own story in the narratives of scripture. If this is so, how can Hebrews offer new lenses through which we relearn to live in and be formed by a world that is Jesus-shaped and cross-centred?

- Hebrews uses stories from Israel's past to show its readers the centrality of Christ and the need to obey – 'Do not do as your fathers did in the wilderness.' What would it look like to use that same logic and use our own histories to make a case for why total obedience in faith is the only viable option for Christians today?

- Fear and persecution were threatening to damage the faith and identity of the recipients of this letter, maybe for good. The pandemic of Covid-19 has shown us that fear of death continues to be a constant threat to the faith. What other fears threaten to speak louder in our churches, such that keeping one's eyes fixed on Christ is difficult or nearly impossible? What resources does the church have to overcome such fears?

- In which ways could the themes of suffering and perseverance in Hebrews help today's Christians rethink and fight against a culture of nominalism, comfort and prosperity?

1 On the humanity of the great high priest

Hebrews 4:14—5:10

The author of Hebrews begs his listeners to come to a deeper understanding of Jesus. It is a matter of life or death for them – and for us. These last verses in Hebrews 4 open the central arguments about Christ in the letter – a discourse on Christology that extends to chapter 7. Hebrews contains both the highest Christology and the lowest – a seesaw of arguments for Christ's divinity and exaltation on the one hand, and expositions of his humanity and suffering on the other. The truth is, however, that Hebrews defies such categorisations of 'high' or 'low'. The author holds both divinity and humanity in equal tension.

There is both a salvific and missional impetus in understanding Jesus' divinity and humanity – we keep our eyes on the fullness of Christ because he is the 'source of eternal salvation' (5:9) and because only through him can we approach the throne and 'find grace to help in time of need' (4:16). The community that holds fast (4:14) in obedience to Christ is a powerful witness in a hostile world.

For us, the term 'high priest' may evoke images of senior clergy officiating at royal weddings or Easter services. Pomp and circumstance, but not much sorrow or flesh-and-blood struggles. In Hebrews, the title 'priest' is 'mingled with the imagery of royal enthronement' from Psalm 110 (Johnson, p. 49). Here, we get a masterful combination of royal settings and deep, human feelings and pain. The author introduced the term in 2:17 and 3:1 and, as we noted, it is unique in the New Testament.

In Judaism the priest had two main roles – a liturgical one, serving as a bridge between God and the people by offering sacrifices for thanksgiving and forgiveness of sins; and a pastoral role, caring for the people and interceding on their behalf. Ordinary priests, even the high priest, had to ask forgiveness for their own sins. This passage in Hebrews reflects these two roles of Jesus, showing also how he perfects them as the one and final priest – no other is necessary. Jesus is fully human, feeling, hurting, suffering and dying like us. He is also fully divine, having been raised from the dead and exalted to God's throne. When Hebrews calls Jesus 'Son' (4:14; 5:5, 8), 'it means this in the fullest possible sense: Jesus is and does what God does' (Johnson, p. 51). Exalted, he is in God's inner courtroom and continues the work of salvation for us.

2 'We shall overcome!'

The last verses of chapter 5 describe a classroom full of petty, immature children, who have heard the best lessons, had excellent teachers and been offered good food, but who have not learned even the basics of how to eat properly. It is a grave image that exposes the lack of understanding and justice in the community and its tendency to revert to old customs. My father used to say, 'A lot of people say they love Jesus and believe in him. The real question is whether they take God seriously.' This is what the author is warning us about in this striking passage.

It is great that they experienced all the joys and wonders of the faith when they first believed (6:1–5), but these will be of no good to them if they remain stagnant. The journey of discipleship requires us to press forward, learning the deep truths about the faith and what it means to say our allegiance is with Jesus, the great high priest.

The recipients of Hebrews, and perhaps many Christians today, seemed to think complacency, immaturity and mediocrity were an optional way to express one's faith. Hebrews 6:6–8 paints a grim picture of the results of stagnation – destruction and death. If Hebrews was written to be delivered orally, as a sermon, one can almost hear the speaker's voice get louder and deeper in this section, a PowerPoint slide of a burning field on the screen. However, the author is not trying to scare his audience into belief. Quite the opposite – we have already learned that because of Christ our fear of death has been overcome (2:15). The question here is, 'What are we going to do with this faith we have been given?' The only option is to persevere and grow deeply into this new life with Christ.

The final verses in chapter 6 describe this life: working out of justice and love for the sake of Christ (6:10), being diligent in displaying our hope (6:11), being not sluggish but imitators of the saints (6:12). The book of Revelation uses the term 'overcomers' to describe those who receive the blessings of God's promises because they have endured persecution and been steadfast in their faith. Likewise in Hebrews, the author is calling his people to overcome. They are able to do so because of God's fidelity to his promises and because our hope is based on the high priest who lives and works in the inner room of God's throne (6:19).

3 Melchizedek and the order of things

They say that in every Alfred Hitchcock film there is at least one cameo appearance of Hitchcock himself. For the author of Hebrews, working as hard as he can to persuade his listeners that Jesus is the great, royal high priest, who is worthy of total obedience and faith, a lot hinges on his use of Psalm 110. He has already quoted from the psalm in Hebrews 5:6, 10 and 6:20. The challenge is that Melchizedek is one of these 'cameo appearance' type of characters in the Bible. He only shows up in Genesis 14 and (drum roll!) Psalm 110. The author has just warned his people about learning and growing in knowledge of the scriptures and faith, so it is almost as though he now needs to show them that he also is learning and growing. So what to make of Melchizedek?

After a brief comment about his name, which in Hebrew means both 'king' (*melech*) of justice (*zedek*) and of peace (*shalom*), the writer makes clear that Melchizedek is not a priest because of his genealogy. On the contrary, he is a priest before the priestly order of the tribe of Levi even existed! We know from the gospel narratives that the religious leaders accused Jesus and his friends of disobeying the religious purity laws, sabbath regulations and even laws on worship and temple attendance. There was an order to things, but the arrival of Messiah Jesus disrupted this order. Here, the author of Hebrews strengthens his argument for Jesus' rightful place as divine Son of God and royal priest by finding in scripture a precedent in Melchizedek.

To be a priest in the order of Melchizedek implies superiority over the Levitical priests. It also means that 'Jesus has made the present Temple and all that goes with it redundant... so discovering what the Psalm meant when talking of the Messiah as a priest as well as a king, is a way to increase and deepen our sense of trust and assurance' in Jesus (Wright, pp. 72–73).

4 Radical inclusiveness and a better hope

Hebrews 7:11–28

A lens which may help us better understand this rather technical passage is that of God's grand plan for creation and the new reality inaugurated by Jesus. Just as the author of Hebrews introduced his argument with 'Long ago God spoke', here we learn a little more of the big story in between then and now. The author continues with the theme of priesthood according to the order of Melchizedek but draws our attention to that perfection (v. 11) which was the intended goal of the grand plan in the first place.

Jesus is indeed superior to those priests who received their priesthood according to the flesh (because they were descendants of the tribe of Levi). Jesus received his priesthood from God himself, and it is one that is both royal and eternal. Furthermore, Christ is able to accomplish that which ordinary priests cannot, because he is also blameless. The priests of the old order, the law and everything that preceded the cross and resurrection of Christ served their purpose in God's plan, but they all pointed forward to Jesus, just as Psalm 110 says. The author of Hebrews is arguing with his listeners to show them that it makes no sense to return to the former ways under the law of Moses and to trust in the priests of the temple, because they cannot bring about the perfection which God intended. Rather, they themselves point to Jesus as the only one who can do that. So trust in this Jesus!

Jesus lives and acts forever on behalf of all (v. 25), granting every person access to the throne of grace (4:16). He is also the one who brings about the new reality, our life in God's future. 'Hope is not a sentiment, but a discipline,' said Willie Jennings in a podcast about the Black Lives Matter protests. This echoes Hebrews. The Christian life must reflect this disciplined hope that only Christ makes possible. The physical realities of temple and law are shown to be less real precisely because they are both temporal and incapable of carrying out the work of perfection. N.T. Wright calls this perfection the 'completeness' of creation (p. 74) – it is the fullness of God's kingdom with all its justice and peace (remember the name 'Melchizedek') that has come in Jesus. There is a radical inclusiveness to this kingdom and to this vision of 'people of God' because, like the order of priests, it is not based on birth or ethnicity or status, but on Christ's work before God's throne.

5 A people of the covenant

Over the next few chapters, the author of Hebrews paints images of heaven and earth, the temple in Jerusalem and the heavenly city, and the tabernacle in the desert. Reading these texts is like looking at artist M.C. Escher's sketches of staircases and rooms that overlap and lead up and down and sideways all at the same time. The author of Hebrews plays with our notions of space and time in a similar way, all along quoting from scripture. It can blow your mind!

Hebrews is also reflecting on what is really real, just as we saw in previous passages. There is a tendency to think of heaven as that which is non-physical, spiritual, a completely different realm. But here the author draws on the Jewish understanding that in the temple (and earlier, the tabernacle), especially in the holy of holies, heaven and earth touched. 'Heaven' simply names God's realm which touches earth in all sorts of ways, not least because earth is part of God's creation. The very physical Jesus – the one who suffered and died and rose again – fully inhabits the heavenly throne, and it is that which is truly real. What Hebrews' listeners have in the earthly temple is only a shadow of what is real in God's realm, so it is inhabiting that realm, through faith in Jesus, that needs to be the focus of the people.

Verses 6–13 are a key part of the letter's argument. Scholars have noted that the word 'better' occurs more times in Hebrews than the rest of the New Testament combined. Hebrews wants its listeners to understand that what they had in the laws of Moses, the old covenants and promises of being God's people, are all good things, but they all point to something better, which is more real, more hopeful and more truthful than anything before. Moreover, this better covenant that refers to Christ's kingdom was already there in scripture, hence the longest single section of quotations in Hebrews (vv. 8–12).

Like the overcomers in Revelation, who will not need a light in the heavenly Jerusalem because Christ will be their light, Hebrews describes the people of this better covenant as those who belong to God (v. 10), who are mature in their faith (v. 11; note the allusion to learning as mature adults from 5:11–14) and whose sins are forgotten (v. 12). It is this picture of God's people that is really real and into which all are called.

6 What we did while we waited

The Covid-19 pandemic triggered ongoing debates as to the best response: governments and health officials arguing and struggling to make plans for how to ease lockdown measures and slowly bring back some sense of 'normal' to daily life. These plans were ever changing, never perfect or final. Even with the prospect of a vaccine, there would still be signs of chaos and confusion, complex special measures and laws that people needed to keep in order to stay safe.

In these early verses of Hebrews 9, the author details some of the special measures that had been in place for God's people while they awaited the coming Messiah and the fulfilment of God's promises. Hebrews elaborates once more on some of the physical aspects of the earthly tabernacle and temple. The spaces painted here are a bit easier to imagine because they are familiar. But, the author argues, just because they are here and they work temporarily does not mean that they are the completion of God's plan. This temple and these priests are not the ones to set things right; they are mere signs of that plan for perfection that we have already heard of (7:11). The things the priests did in the tabernacle or in the temple were just holding measures, things Israel did while it waited for Christ's coming. Even as holding measures, they were extremely important because, as we have seen in the previous chapter, they pointed to Jesus and to the coming of the ultimate high priest.

Hebrews is preparing its hearers once again for the whole point of the letter, which we will see in the following section: Christ has come. There is a complete and perfect vaccine that is available for all immediately, so why are you still living as if under lockdown?

Guidelines

One of the big challenges that the entire book of Hebrews offers to Christians today has to do with learning and growth. The author demands much of his readers, not just in terms of perseverance during times of persecution, but also in terms of real deep growth in the faith. In many places today there is very little teaching or preaching that suggests our very lives are in danger if we don't learn more about Christ. Understanding Christology, eschatology, etc. is not just something for the experts or academic theologians. Rather, the gospel demands that we think, pray and live in ways that reflect the depth of faith in Jesus.

- Learning and growing in the faith is not simply an intellectual exercise. Rather, it is looking at the world and our societies today and working out what are the issues that are tearing us apart, that divide and threaten communities. Then it is asking one another: how can we deal with this in a manner that is faithful to scripture? What are the issues in our contexts that require as much thought and action as those the author of Hebrews asks of his people?

- The initial recipients of Hebrews thought that it was necessary to maintain certain practices, forms of worship and identity markers in order to be properly seen as God's people. Like them, we also tend to think that we know what it means to be the people of God and what counts or not as 'Christian'. Hebrews challenges us to think of the ways our identity markers and worship practices are shaped by understandings of race, history, gender, economics, etc. as it offers us a vision of God's people shaped by 'the better covenant' (8:6) of cross and resurrection. What would a new conversion to this radical new age inaugurated by Christ look like in our churches today?

1 The waiting is over: 'Behold the lamb who sits on the throne'

Hebrews 9:11—10:18

All that the people have planned and hoped for, all they have waited for, has come – God and his kingdom made real in the person of Jesus. Yet persecution and challenges remain, so the author of Hebrews argues that, though the people cannot yet see all of God's new world, they can see Jesus and they can be certain that this new reality is much, much better than anything that came before it. As he has already pointed out, all that came before was actually a foretaste of the reality inaugurated by Jesus. Under the old covenant, the priests entered the temple daily and the high priest entered the holy of holies annually to offer (imperfect) sacrifices for the people. Now Jesus is alive and active forever before the throne of God and has offered himself as the perfect sacrifice (9:12, 14). He is both the sacrificial lamb and the one who sits on the throne.

Throughout this passage, the theme of completeness or perfection appears in relation to the sacrifice of Christ on the cross. Christians today often struggle with the language of sacrifice and blood offerings, but what is key here is to understand these in the context of the Day of Atonement in Israel's story. The sacrifices offered for the sins of the people were both a sign from the people to God and of God's love for the people. The Greek word for 'will' and 'covenant' are the same (9:15–18). God has written his will and made promises to his heirs. Just as someone needs to die in order for the heirs to receive their share, so here God needs to die for the inheritance to be passed along to God's children. In history there were many days of atonement, but there was only one day on which Jesus died. His death 'at the end of the age' (9:26) indicates precisely this meaning of completion – all of history has been perfected, completed in this one sacrifice, annulling the need for any future sacrifices.

Hebrews draws on Psalm 40 to show once more how the cultic language of the past pointed forward to the ultimate reality of Christ's sacrifice. His readers might want to go back to their old ways, but they need to understand that the old law will not save them. The idea that God would become human and die is scandalous. It was an obstacle then, as it is today. This text not only argues for why it was necessary for God's Son to die, but also shows that it was all along part of God's plan to redeem and make all creation complete once more.

2 Blessed are those persecuted for the sake of righteousness

Hebrews 10:19-39

All of Hebrews has been about Messiah Jesus. The arguments have been stacking up for how the old laws, the psalms and the prophets pointed towards this culmination of God's loving plan towards humanity. Jesus is not only the perfect high priest who also offers himself as the perfect sacrifice, but he is also the one who enables us to appear before God. The only proper response to this is worship.

Initially, the author takes on a more pastoral tone, calling his readers 'friends' and encouraging them in the character they need to develop in order to worship rightly this Jesus they have met and about whom they now know much more. In chapter 8, we learned some of the characteristics of God's people through the words of Jeremiah. Here, these are called to mind again – it is not simply a matter of intellectual assent to Jesus, but it is having God's law on our hearts and minds so that we are pure and blameless, filled with a better hope because we have glimpsed this new reality and it has become real for us as individuals and as community. This witnessing character of the faith is also a key theme in this passage. It matters a great deal how we talk to one another, how we show our love and generosity and how we persevere in these good things despite the circumstances.

As we saw in earlier sections of Hebrews, here again comes the advisory against failure to follow Christ. It is not a scare tactic by the author, but a careful explanation about judgement – how it worked under the old law and how it still works under Christ. The new reality of Christ brings not only the perfection and completion of sacrifice and a better covenant; it also brings perfect judgement. God's love and faithfulness are not undermined by punishment for turning away from God's grace. Rather, because Jesus is the only blameless and faithful high priest, he is also the only true judge. His judgements are just and perfect.

Remember your first love and how it caused you to act and think rightly. Once more the author is begging his people to persevere as they had in the past. This has implications for how they act as individuals and together, holding one another up for the sake of Christ and God's mission. Endure and do not fall back, because the loving Jesus is also the just judge.

3 The faith of fathers and mothers

Hebrews 11:1–22

The author of Hebrews wants his listeners to hear the story of God, how it overlaps with their own, and to realise that in Jesus they have witnessed the unfolding of the divine drama, just as their ancestors had hoped for.

In chapter 2, Hebrews already made the case that suffering is 'the means by which Jesus reaches the perfection that enables him to save' (Johnson, p. 53). As the author urges the people to remain faithful in their path of discipleship, he here reminds them that their fathers and mothers also suffered hardships, persecution and threat of loss of land and family, yet they remained faithful to the hope of the promises of God.

Perhaps part of the challenge that the recipients of this letter were facing concerned their identity and sense of belonging. If they were mostly Jewish Christians, they fit in neither in the synagogue nor in a Gentile setting. It is destabilising and difficult not to belong. To help with this, the author takes his readers back to the stories of their ancestors to show that indeed they do belong to a long line of faithful people who overcame their own struggles in order to obey God. If anything, the readers should not doubt their identity, but remain and grow even stronger in it, knowing that they are heirs of the promises. To explain this further, Hebrews makes the explicit link between faith and hope (v. 1) and between the God who created everything and the God of the particular promises to Abraham and Sarah and their descendants (vv. 3, 8–12). Christians are equipped with this hopeful faith, and it is the tool that enables all to press forward in discipleship, trusting that the God of all creation is also the God who fulfils the promises to his children.

4 The faith of communities

While the faith of particular heroes and heroines from the past is of utmost significance, it is also necessary to remember their stories in connection with the communities and people of which they were a part. Moses' faith is displayed not only in the way he gave up a privileged life in Pharaoh's household, but also in how he learned to be the leader of the people that God wanted him to be. In Hebrews 4, the author reminded his readers that we need one another as we follow the path set by Jesus. Moses, as we know from Exodus 2, was not going about God's work as he should have, but with help he not only remained faithful but, even more so, was used by God to confront Pharaoh and to lead the people out of Egypt. Hebrews attributes Moses' faithfulness to his prophetic understanding of Christ (v. 26). If Moses was willing to suffer abuse and persecution by the king of Egypt, how much more should the readers of Hebrews be willing to endure their present sufferings! They, like Moses, must keep their eyes on Jesus in order to do so.

One can read back into the list of people and communities in Hebrews 11:29–39 Tertullian's famous saying, 'The blood of martyrs is the seed of the Church' (*Apologeticus*). Tertullian was making the case for why Christianity should have the same legal status as other sects within the Roman empire. Part of his argument was that the more Christians were killed, the more they would multiply and grow. There is this same idea in this passage of Hebrews – God's people endured horrible things in the past because they had faith in God's promises and hope for the coming reality of God's reign. But unlike those who were martyred in the past, the people of Hebrews have been blessed to see God's promises fulfilled because they have seen Jesus (2:9). As was argued in chapter 2, there is still suffering and death, but those who follow in faith, whether in the past or present, are themselves beacons of the new reality that God is bringing about for the restoration of creation. Suffering is the way of discipleship. If the people turn back to their old ways, they will be trampling on the very people who paved the way for them in the first place.

5 Big shoes to fill

One way to picture the argument of Hebrews is as a spiral staircase. At each floor the author describes something from Israel's past, such as the laws of Moses, the sacrificial system or the lives of their ancestors. Then the stairs circle around to the main point that these various descriptions have been leading to – Jesus the promised Messiah. At each conclusion the author gives us another view or angle by which we see Jesus as the fulfilment of what has gone before.

Here, we return again to the point of suffering and the faith of those who endured. If they thought their heroes and heroines had suffered terribly and shown great faith and trust in God, how much more should they then consider the sufferings of Jesus? Christ is not only able and worthy to fill the shoes of people like Abraham and Moses, but he is also the one who makes perfect all they tried to do. The imagery used is that of a race. The cloud of witnesses are Abraham, Sarah, Rahab and the many saints, who are in the stands cheering and encouraging us to persevere. Faith requires discipline and practice for it to strengthen and grow. Building on the imagery that the people are in the long line of God's children, they need also to understand that, as a wise parent, God uses different means and ways to correct and to show the limits within which we are to live.

At the end of the race, those who have received God's grace and persevered enter into the new Jerusalem, Mount Zion (v. 22). There is once more a dramatic contrast made between the old mountain, Sinai, and the new one, Zion, which is also the new temple. In Exodus, Mount Sinai is clouded in fear and darkness and threatens all who approach it. The new reality of God's reign is one where we are welcomed as children to the mountain of God. We can approach it with thankful hearts because we have been made pure and holy by the blood of Jesus. The promise of God's new world is also a warning that, in God's time, the old earth and the old heavens will pass away (v. 27); therefore we must be prepared for the new.

6 Learning to share, endure, pray and bid farewell

Throughout the letter of Hebrews, the author has been making the point that Jesus – fully God and fully human – is the one of whom the psalms spoke and the one whom Moses saw in the future. It is this same Jesus who the readers must see by faith so that they endure and come to see him face-to-face when they have finished their race. With their focus on this Jesus, they must learn to order their daily lives as individuals and as a community so that they reflect and witness to the faith and hope they have in Christ. 'The practical life of the Christian community must be ordered in such a way that generosity and love – the love… that reflects and continues to embody God's own self-giving love – will be its central feature' (Wright, p. 169). Believers must learn to help one another pray and to look after those in prison, recognising that persecution and imprisonment are very real outcomes of faithful discipleship.

As the people of God, they must stand out from the cultures around them. This was central then as much as it is today. Living lives worthy of the gospel of Christ has everything to do with how married couples witness to Christ's love, how the church and all its members handle financial matters and look after the poor.

There are more clues about the recipients of this letter in these final verses than anywhere else in Hebrews. The author contrasts their citizenship with those who live presently in Jerusalem. His readers belong to the heavenly Jerusalem, so they should expect to meet outside the city walls. They should expect persecution, recognising that by claiming a heavenly citizenship they will be seen as threats to the powers of the present age.

Much of Hebrews has focused on the death of Jesus as the perfect sacrifice – the one anticipated by all the history and rituals of Israel. In his suffering and death, God inaugurated a new reality, and we have glimpses of God's new world because of faith in Jesus. In verse 20 the author makes explicit what he has assumed all along – the power of God demonstrated in the resurrection. The climax of God's story with his creation is made complete, perfected in the cycle of the suffering, death and resurrection of Jesus. So with eyes fixed on this Jesus, we are enabled to run the race for his glory.

Guidelines

- The character and content of hope is a key theme in Hebrews. What are some practices for Christians today that would enable us to live in a way that more fully demonstrates the content of this better hope?

- How do the daily goings-on of churches today express the new reality of God's just and peaceful kingdom inaugurated by Jesus?

- 'Hebrews challenges present-day sensibilities... by seeing suffering as the very heart of discipleship... It is the very path by which humans become transformed, as was Jesus, into fully mature children of God' (Johnson, p. 60). In a culture that does everything possible to avoid suffering, what are the implications for taking Hebrews seriously in the church today? Perhaps one significant way to rethink understandings of suffering is to pay closer attention to Christians who are persecuted around the world today. What could it mean for our daily lives if we considered how profound it is that we are part of the same body of Christ with those who are shot at and beheaded for their faith?

FURTHER READING

Sean Gladding, *The Story of God, the Story of Us: Getting lost and found in the Bible* (IVP, 2010).

Willie James Jennings, 'My Anger, God's Righteous Indignation: Response to the death of George Floyd': podcast, *For the Life of the World*, 2 June 2020.

Luke Timothy Johnson, *Hebrews: A commentary* (Westminster John Knox Press, 2006).

Tom Wright, *Hebrews for Everyone* (SPCK, 2004).

Ezra

Pauline Hoggarth

'For we are slaves; yet our God has not forsaken us in our slavery, but has extended to us his steadfast love…to give us new life' (Ezra 9:9). Ezra's heartfelt prayer goes to the heart of the narrative that carries his name, the good news that because of God's committed love, the past never has the last word and the possibilities of newness are unfailing. Beyond the catastrophe of conquest, destruction and exile, God's people could imagine, and work towards, recovery – and Ezra would help shape that process.

In the Hebrew scriptures, the books of Ezra and Nehemiah, which we read later in the year, are one consecutive narrative. They continue the story told in Chronicles (the closing verses of 2 Chronicles are almost identical with the opening verses of Ezra), but almost certainly have a different author. It is likely that Ezra himself brought together at some point in the fifth century BC a variety of sources, including his own memoirs recorded in chapters 7—10. The two 'movements' of the book (1:1—6:22 and 7:1—10:44) describe two separate Jewish migrations from Persia to Judah for the purposes of reconstruction. The first, around 538BC, was led by Zerubbabel (2:2) and focused on the rebuilding of the Jerusalem temple, destroyed by the Babylonians in 586BC. The second, some 80 years later and led by Ezra himself (7:1–6), sought the rebuilding of a community identity shaped by God's word.

As I reflect on these chapters in early 2020, the world is reeling from the impact of coronavirus. Visions of recovery compete with one another from country to country; leadership is under scrutiny; people demand to know where, if anywhere, is God in all this. Might Ezra's story of recovery offer insights?

Unless otherwise stated, Bible quotations are taken from the NRSV. Author references are to works in the 'Further reading' list.

1 God the stirrer

The nature of the God we believe in will shape the character and direction of our lives. Do we think of the Lord as an impassive, domesticated observer of the world he has made, irrelevant to human activity? Or as an active, involved and sometimes disturbing presence? The opening chapter of Ezra implies the second characterisation. Twice the narrator describes God as an initiating force in historical events, as he 'stirred up the spirit' – first of King Cyrus of Persia (v. 1) and then of some of the Jewish community leaders living in exile in Babylonia (v. 5). The outcome of this divine disturbance would be the rebuilding of the Jerusalem temple and the restoration there of normal worship (vv. 2–4). The narrator underlines the boldness of these claims by his reference to Jeremiah's prophecies (v. 1), though scholars debate exactly which ones (Jeremiah 29:10 and 51:11, for example).

The book of Ezra is unashamedly *theological* history. The British Museum's 'Cyrus Cylinder' suggests a different interpretation of these events. Discovered in 1879 in Mesopotamia (modern Iraq), this document, impressed in clay, dates from around 539BC. The text makes no mention of the Jews or Jerusalem but claims that Cyrus 'repatriated all exiled communities in Babylon without distinction, and provided for the restoration of their deities to their temples' (McConville, p. 8). In other words, Cyrus' edict was the strategy of a shrewd and pragmatic politician who believed, along with other early Persian kings, that gods other than their own Marduk must be placated (see, for example, Artaxerxes' concern in 7:23). The narrator emphasises his understanding of God's character as rescuer and redeemer in the unmistakeable echoes of the Egyptian exodus in his story (vv. 4, 6; compare Exodus 11:2–3; 12:35–36). In addition to the freewill offerings of their Gentile neighbours, the returnees would take with them the rich furnishings of the Jerusalem temple, stolen by Nebuchadnezzar in 587BC (2 Chronicles 36:18) and now carefully inventoried and released by Cyrus and his administrators (vv. 7–11).

The detailed list of the returnees in chapter 2 is replicated almost exactly in Nehemiah 7:6–73. The implication of verse 5 is that not all the people entitled by Cyrus' edict to return to Jerusalem did in fact do so; the ones who did were, in theological terms, those who responded to God's prompting. But the process almost certainly involved the same kind of prudent evaluation as Cyrus' edict. After almost 70 years since the exile to Babylon, many of these people would know nothing of their homeland.

2 Mixed feelings

Ezra 3

The returnees listed in chapter 2 scattered to different communities in Judah ('the towns', 2:70; 3:1), but the seventh month of that first year (September/October 538BC) drew them together to Jerusalem to celebrate the 'ingathering' or festival of booths (3:4). This harvest festival, Sukkot, was one of three annual commemorations that God ordained for his people after their rescue from Egypt (Exodus 23:16; Leviticus 23:34–36). Never had it been more important for a dispersed population to come together in worship and the recognition that each individual belonged to a wider community with a common memory, first of the liberation of their ancestors from Egypt some eight centuries earlier and then of their recent return from Babylonian exile. The highlight of the festival of booths was the building of rough shelters from branches and greenery in which people camped out for a week – a reminder of their precarious existence after the exodus (Leviticus 23:40–43).

The preparations for a return to normality started with the rebuilding of the altar on the remains of its foundations at the heart of the temple precinct and the renewal of offerings 'as prescribed in the law of Moses the man of God' (v. 2; verses 2 and 3 act as a flashback). The people's emotions are a juxtaposition of 'dread of the neighbouring peoples' (v. 3) and generosity in support of the temple rebuilding (vv. 5, 7). The nature of the opposition will be detailed in the following chapter.

The work of reconstruction and recovery moves outwards from the altar as the focus of worship to the start of work on the foundations of the temple itself (vv. 8, 10). The place echoes with joyful responsive singing in praise of God's unchanging love for his people. For the older generation, though, this was a day of mixed emotions. Rightly or wrongly, they made negative comparisons with the glories of the past of which they had been eyewitnesses (v. 12). The narrator reports the mixed response, the generational differences, but the younger generation's shout of joy wins the day. It was 'heard far away', out where hostile forces were planning the opposition that is the subject of the next chapter. In any recovery project, leaders need wisdom to cope with different expectations, different visions of what 'success' will look like. Zerubbabel must have been glad, at this dangerous moment, of the encouragement of the prophet Haggai, with his understanding of people's feelings and his bracing call from the Lord to 'take courage… work, for I am with you… My spirit abides among you' (Haggai 2:4–5).

3 Facing discouragement

Ezra 4

The three chapters that conclude the first 'movement' of Ezra (4—6) describe how the people persevered with, and finally completed, the building of the Jerusalem temple in the face of various kinds of opposition. The construction took over 20 years, and it is only in 6:15 that completion is mentioned. The structure of these chapters is complicated. The narrator-editor has gathered different accounts of opposition to the building programme and put them together with little regard to chronology. Verses 1–5 and 24 refer to events from the period 536–520BC – a suspect offer of help during early construction of the altar and temple followed by bribery of Persian officials that led to all work being halted. The section of narrative framed by the start of the work and its suspension for 18 years (vv. 6–23) moves the narrative forward some 30 years to 486–460BC, to a different kind of opposition, this time to the rebuilding of the city and its walls (vv. 12, 16).

What lay behind Zerubbabel's bluntly hostile refusal of help from people described as 'adversaries of Judah and Benjamin' but who self-identified as fellow-worshippers of Yahweh (vv. 2–3)? Zerubbabel explains his rejection of help in terms of obedience to Cyrus' decree. His true concern, hinted at in the talk of 'your God' and 'our God', was that those people offering help were still practising the corrupt forms of worship that their ancestors had developed two centuries before, after the fall of Samaria. The story is told in 2 Kings 17, note especially verse 41a. The returned exiles were not to be seduced into assimilation or to be frightened off by what then became more direct attacks that delayed completion of the temple until the time of Darius (vv. 4–5).

Between accounts of opposition to the temple building (vv. 1–5, 24), the focus shifts in verses 6–23 to information about documentary attacks from different sources to the Persian rulers who followed Darius – first an anonymous accusation sent to Ahasuerus/Xerxes, then two to Artaxerxes, who was Ezra's patron (7:6). Artaxerxes sends a reply, withdrawing his support for the rebuilding of the city (vv. 17–22).

Rehum and his associates were skilled in focusing their accusations against the returned exiles on the king's concerns – at this period Persia was involved in an expensive war against the Greeks. They paint a picture of diminished tax returns (v. 13) and the likely takeover of an entire province (v. 16). Boldly, they suggest the king check the history of these people in his own archives (v. 15).

4 Joy!

The first and longer 'movement' of Ezra closes on a note of celebration and thanksgiving to God. Twenty years of starts and delays have culminated in a rebuilt temple and celebration of the Passover.

The narrative of chapter 5 and 6:1–12 picks up the story of the rebuilding of the temple from where it broke off in 4:5. Darius now rules the Persian empire, and three new characters have joined the dramatis personae: the prophets Haggai and Zechariah (5:1; 6:14) and Tattenai, Darius' governor of the empire's western province that included Palestine (5:13).

Tattenai seems to have been a rather different kind of official from the openly hostile and sycophantic Rehum. Tattenai's letter to Darius allows the returnees to make their own case for the rebuilding of the temple (5:11–13). There is little doubt, though, that Tattenai's intention was to halt the building project. How ironic that not only did Darius' research in the Ecbatana archives bring to light Cyrus' original decree permitting the reconstruction, but Tattenai himself is ordered to support the project with money and materials (6:1–12)!

The narrator attributes the renewed security of the building project and the commitment of the people to complete the work to two factors: the watchful and protective eye of God, especially on that archive research (5:5), and the continued influence of the public preaching of two prophets, Haggai and Zechariah (6:14). The messages of both men combined urgent warning with compassionate encouragement – 'My house lies in ruins, while all of you hurry off to your own houses'; 'My spirit abides among you; do not fear' (Haggai 1:9; 2:5); 'Just as, when I called, they would not hear… I scattered them'; 'I will save you and you shall be a blessing. Do not be afraid' (Zechariah 7:13–14; 8:13).

Joy is the characteristic note of this climactic chapter – joy that had its source in the God who had drawn world rulers into his purposes (vv. 14, 22), the joy of a community of people with different histories but a common sense of identity (v. 21), the joy of work completed and dedicated (vv. 16–17) and the joy of return to the normal and familiar temple practices (v. 18). The narrator carefully records the date, the sixth year of Darius' reign, 515BC, 72 years after the destruction of Solomon's temple.

5 'I took courage'

Ezra 7

Some 60 years separate the dedication of the rebuilt temple and the Passover celebration in the reign of Darius from the arrival of Ezra in Jerusalem, probably around 458BC during the reign of Artaxerxes I (465–424BC). The first part of the chapter (vv. 1–10) details Ezra's qualification for leadership of the crucial second part of the recovery project – not now the reconstruction of temple and city but the reshaping of the people as distinctively committed to God's ways. Had Israel truly learned the hard lessons of defeat, destruction and exile? The genealogy of verses 1–4 demonstrates Ezra's priestly credentials through his descent from Aaron. In fact, we will rarely see him in this role because it will be his experience as 'a scribe skilled in the law of Moses' (v. 6) that will be most urgently needed at this time in the Jerusalem community. Crucially, Ezra's scholarly Torah skills are not a matter of mere head learning; God's ways are deep in his heart and evidenced in coherent living and skill in communicating to others (v. 10). The narrator deliberately links God's blessing on Ezra's journey to the quality of his life (vv. 9–10).

Artaxerxes' letter to Ezra (vv. 11–26) was written in response to Ezra's detailed request (v. 6). Indeed, it may have been written by Ezra himself and approved by the king. The 'king of kings' acknowledges 'the God of heaven' and provides his emissary with a comprehensive job description. Ezra will primarily make this journey so as 'to make inquiries about Judah and Jerusalem according to the law of your God' (v. 14). He is to appoint judges and magistrates to enact God's laws, make sure that the people are familiar with them and take measures to discipline rebels (vv. 25–26). In relation to the temple, Ezra will lead a group of new immigrants, mainly destined for service there (v. 7), carry donations from the Persian court and other sources along with new ceremonial vessels for temple worship (vv. 15–20). The extraordinary new element introduced into the narrative is the Persian king's concern, not now only for temple rebuilding and rituals but that God's law should shape the behaviour of his distant citizens – a concern the narrator once more attributes to God's initiative (v. 27).

As the chapter closes Ezra's own voice breaks out in a doxology to the God whose steadfast love has provided the courage he needs for the demanding tasks that lie ahead (vv. 27–28).

6 A time for lament

Ezra 9:1—10:9

Accusations and conspiracy theories have been rife since the outbreak of the coronavirus pandemic. Different groups have been blamed for importing or spreading the disease, or the virus has been identified as God's judgement on certain behaviours – always of others. The outstanding feature of Ezra's response to a most challenging ethical problem is his refusal to point the finger or make accusations. Like other authentic prophets in scripture, Ezra includes himself in confessional lament (9:6–15; compare Isaiah 64:6–9; Daniel 9:3–19). He prayed in solidarity with his community – they all stood in need of God's mercy.

But what prompted Ezra's appalled response (see 9:3)? Did it come as a shock to him, after the problem-free arrival of his delegation in Jerusalem and the faithful discharge of all his tasks (chapter 8), when community leaders voiced their concerns about widespread intermarriage with foreign women (9:1–2)? It is likely that awareness of the problem had grown in the light of Ezra's own teaching of the law in the four months or so since his arrival in Jerusalem (10:9). Now his grief and sense of shame draws out a response from the community. No moralising, no imposition of punishment, but the community's own terrible resolution 'to send away all these wives and their children… according to the law' (10:3).

This closing episode of Ezra's story (we meet him again in the book of Nehemiah) is divisive. We may come from a church culture that applauds a decisive, unapologetic stance on a range of ethical issues, or from one with a strong theology of God's grace, acceptance and welcome of 'the other'. We may ponder the fact that several Old Testament leaders, including Moses and Joseph, married 'foreign' women, and that the apostle Paul encouraged Christians not to marry unbelievers (2 Corinthians 6:14) but directed those with unbelieving partners not to divorce them (1 Corinthians 7:12–16). Nehemiah would face the same problem but did not resort to wholesale separation (Nehemiah 13:23–27). We are not told what happened to the wives and children who were sent away. They may have been provided with certificates of divorce, which would enable the women to remarry (Deuteronomy 24:1–4). Maybe they simply returned to their families like Orpah did (Ruth 1:15). The underlying issue for which Ezra was contending was Israel's distinctiveness: 'Israel's mission could only make headway if she maintained the servant identity that separated her from the nations to whom she should mediate the revelation of God' (Shepherd and Wright, p. 150).

Guidelines

If you have time, it would be good to read the whole of the book of Ezra to build up as complete an understanding as possible of the recovery story and of the person of Ezra as teacher, priest, administrator, intercessor and law-giver.

- How do you understand the portrayal of God in the book of Ezra as a 'stirrer' both of global political power-brokers and of people in the faith community? To what extent do you practise 'political' prayer? How might the Ezra perspective influence your practice?

- Issues of identity were crucial for the post-exilic community in Jerusalem. To what extent do you think this is also true of our contemporary churches? Can we emphasise Christian identity unhelpfully? 'Are new believers being taught to know their identity, to know the people they belong to, to understand their deep roots in the Scriptures (Old as well as New Testaments)… Most evangelistic and discipling programs seem to place their emphasis on solving the problem of the immediate present (my personal sin and need for forgiveness) and the ultimate future (being sure to "go to heaven" when I die)' (Shepherd and Wright, p. 162).

FURTHER READING

David J. Shepherd and Christopher J.H. Wright, *Ezra and Nehemiah* (Eerdmans, 2018).

L. Allen and T. Laniak, *Ezra, Nehemiah, Esther* (Hendrickson Publishers, 2003).

J.G. McConville, *Ezra, Nehemiah, and Esther* (Westminster John Knox Press, 1985).

John Goldingay, *Ezra, Nehemiah and Esther for Everyone* (SPCK, 2012).

Joseph Too Shao and Rosa Ching Shao, *Ezra and Nehemiah: A pastoral and contextual commentary* (Langham Partnership, 2019).

Mark 11—13

Steve Motyer

Welcome back to Mark! We take another three-week break in the Holy Land with Mark as our tour guide – but this time based in Jerusalem, where Jesus arrives at the start of this section. In fact, Jesus has been moving in this direction since Peter's confession in Caesarea Philippi (8:27), which was to the north of Galilee near Mount Hermon, the probable site of the transfiguration (9:2). From there Jesus moved south to Galilee again (9:30), then south again to the area east of the Jordan (10:1), before turning west on the road to Jerusalem (10:32), through Jericho (10:46), and finally to the Mount of Olives, where we pick up the story (11:1).

In chapters 11—13 Jesus acts and teaches in Jerusalem, specifically in the temple, which forms an essential theological backdrop to what happens. The temple was the focus of Israel's relationship with God. Jews living all over the world sent their 'temple tax' to maintain the daily round of worship and sacrifices, and the three main annual festivals (Passover, Tabernacles and the Day of Atonement) attracted huge crowds of pilgrims. It symbolised God's commitment to Israel, and therefore Israel's security. The priests not only conducted the sacrifices – assuring Israel of forgiveness – but also, with the 'scribes', focused the teaching and learning of the law which was at the heart of the relationship with God (compare Luke 2:46).

It is essential to remember all this as we launch into these three chapters. There are shocks and surprises in store. The key uniting theme, against this background, is the arrival of the kingdom of God in Jesus, and the implications and outworking of this – Mark signalled this basic theme back in 1:15. The implications of the arrival of the kingdom are radical indeed, as we will see!

Unless otherwise stated, Bible quotations are my own translation.

1 The coming kingdom

Mark 11:1–10

The alert reader will notice that we are repeating a reading – the so-called 'triumphal entry' concluded our last set of readings in Mark. This is because this is a bridge passage, which both concludes the section of teaching about the kingdom, starting with Peter's 'confession' in 8:29, and leads into the next section based in Jerusalem, which Jesus finally enters in 11:11.

The question 'What kind of kingdom does Jesus bring?' is the vital one for Mark (and for us). The Mount of Olives (v. 1) was a rallying point for aspiring Messiahs – Josephus the Jewish historian tells us that 'the Egyptian', referred to in Acts 21:38 as the leader of a revolt against Rome, started his rebellion by declaring that he was a prophet and calling people to join him on the Mount of Olives (Josephus, *Antiquities* 20:169). So the disciples' shout in verse 10, 'Blessed is the coming kingdom of our father David!', has revolutionary over-tones – even though Jesus does not stop on the Mount of Olives, but enters the Holy City: David's son (see 10:47–48) arriving in David's city.

So what did his disciples mean as they heralded his 'coming kingdom'? Did they think that Jesus was about to set up a new earthly kingdom like David's? Peter's resistance to the idea of a *suffering* and *dying* Messiah after his confession (8:32) suggests this is what he thought at that point. But has he changed? If we asked him now, 'What kind of Davidic king is Jesus?', what would he say?

Mark leaves this open, and thus faces his readers with the same question. It sounds like Jesus' arrival is good news – 'Hosanna in the highest!' (v. 10) – but the disciples' other cry, 'Blessed is the one who comes in the name of the Lord!' (v. 9), was a regular greeting addressed to all pilgrims. Is Jesus more than this? In what ways might his arrival be different from that of all other pilgrims? The donkey incident (vv. 1–6) hints at specialness – a feature which Matthew and John develop, commenting that it fulfils Zechariah 9:9 (Matthew 21:1–5; John 12:14–15). But Mark keeps quiet about this link, leaving it to his readers to spot the connection and draw conclusions.

So as we move into the next section of the gospel, the question is press-ing – with what kind of visibility and power does God's kingdom arrive with Jesus? This question is just as vital today for the church of Christ.

2 The fruitless tree

What an anticlimax verse 11 is! The Davidic King arrives in his temple uncelebrated. No crowds, no trumpets, no welcome. Instead, a cool inspection: 'looked around' is a favourite verb of Mark's – see for example 3:5; 10:23 – and has the idea of 'looking with significant attention'. What does the King see? We discover the result of his inspection the next day, when Jesus returns to the temple and starts throwing out the traders (vv. 15–18).

But first we read the strange story of the cursing of the fig tree, blamed for not having any fruit even though, as Mark explains, 'it was not the time for figs' (vv. 13–14). It is not surprising that readers rise up in defence of the tree. Is Jesus acting unreasonably?

The reference may be to the small green early figs which formed over winter and were sometimes picked and eaten in the spring after the leaves appeared. In this case, Jesus might well have expected to find figs just because he saw leaves. But this still falls foul of Mark's comment that Jesus found only leaves 'because it was not the time for figs'. Another explanation – perhaps a better one – is that this is autumn, not spring, and Jesus approaches the tree hoping that the figs have not yet been harvested – but there is nothing left. No harvest remaining. Mark's comment would then mean 'for the time for harvesting the figs was past'. This autumn date would fit with the Tabernacles-style actions by the disciples in 11:8, and with the impression Mark will give in chapter 12 (and in 14:49) that Jesus spent quite some time teaching in the temple before his arrest at Passover.

But the vital thing is the meaning of this action, and here the prophet Micah comes to our aid, supporting an autumn setting as he does so: in Micah 7:1–2 God says, 'Woe is me! For I have become like one who, after the summer fruit has been gathered… finds no cluster to eat; there is no first-ripe fig for which I hunger. The faithful have disappeared from the land, and there is no one left who is upright' (NRSV). There is nothing left for the Lord, hungering for the faith of his people. It is highly likely that this Micah passage was in Mark's mind, and possibly also in Jesus', as he enacts a parable that pictures the dramatic action about to follow.

3 A place of prayer for all!

Again Jesus heads for the temple on entering Jerusalem, and must have amazed – even scandalised? – his disciples by his attack on the temple trade (v. 15). The vast Court of the Gentiles (500 yards by 350, enclosed by a magnificent portico) was an ideal place for traders to supply pilgrims with what they needed for their worship: in many cases, a dove to sacrifice, and the means to buy it in the prescribed temple currency, the 'shekel of the sanctuary' (see Exodus 30:13). For the wealthier worshipper, there were also lambs on sale.

Mark does not say that Jesus was attacking *corruption* in the temple, although his reference to the 'den of thieves' (v. 17, quoting Jeremiah 7:11) might suggest this was part of the problem. Rather, this is an assault on the temple system itself. These traders were there to be helpful, to enable the worship to take place. Jesus seeks to stop it. 'And he would not let anyone carry sacred vessels through the temple' – this is probably the right translation, and understanding, of the strange verse 16. *Jesus acts symbolically to bring the temple system to a halt!*

Why? Verse 17 summarises the teaching he then gives, focusing on a quotation of Isaiah 56:7, 'My house shall be called a house of prayer for all the nations.' Jesus does three incredibly bold and dramatic things here: he lays claim to the temple – this is 'my house', his ownership signalled by his dramatic action. He opens the temple up to 'all the Gentiles' (people knew that Gentiles were not allowed further into the temple, beyond the outer court). And he specifies that the temple is for 'prayer', i.e. only for prayer, and not for offering sacrifices.

Dramatic indeed! Sacrifices are about buying animals and performing rituals; prayer is about a real heart-connection and *metanoia* (1:15: repentance, life-change) before God. Jeremiah's 'den of thieves' accusation was about precisely this. The people were trusting that all God wants is the outward 'doing' of the ceremonies in the prescribed place, so that they can carry on living wickedly with a clear conscience and no desire to reform. As a result, Jeremiah predicted the destruction of the temple (Jeremiah 7:1–15). Jesus will do the same in Mark 13.

People liked this teaching (v. 18)! But the authorities, who ran the temple, did not. Once again Jesus leaves the Holy City (v. 19). No home for him there.

4 The place and power of prayer

Mark 11:20–25

Mark has a favourite storytelling device which we meet here. Known as the 'sandwich technique', it involves dividing a story into two parts around a middle section to which the surrounding story relates in some telling way. The most famous example is the raising of Jairus' daughter, within which the healing of the 'unclean' woman is sandwiched (Mark 5:21–43). There are other notable instances at 3:20–35 and 14:1–11.

So here we resume the story of the fig tree, now completely dead (v. 20), and Peter makes the connection with Jesus' curse (v. 21). Clearly Mark wants us to see the fig tree as a parable or illustration of what Jesus has just done to the temple (vv. 15–19). Has Jesus effectively just judged, cursed and destroyed the temple? Many think that this story looks forward to Jesus' prediction of the destruction of the temple in chapter 13, and there must be some truth in this.

But maybe the message is not entirely negative. The passion with which he overturned the tables was not anger at corruption, as we saw, but anger that, in its present set-up which emphasised the distinction between Israel and the Gentiles – restricting the Gentiles to the outer court – the temple could not fulfil God's universal vision of 'a house of prayer for all nations' (v. 17). In Micah's words, the Lord comes looking for that fruit, and that faith is not to be found. Structured in that way, the temple simply cannot sustain that faith.

Against this background, Jesus' words in verses 22–25 are so telling. The place of prayer is not now the temple but wherever 'you stand' (v. 25a). And the place of forgiveness is not now the temple – with its elaborate prescriptions of sacrifices for sins – but the praying heart which forgives others as we simply ask our heavenly Father for forgiveness for ourselves (v. 25b). No need for doves or sheep. And the vital condition of effective prayer is not now obedient participation in temple worship, but simply 'faith in God' (v. 22), which has miracle-working power (v. 23). And the 'you' for whom all this is true – 'you' plural, even though Peter alone asks the implicit question in verse 21 – is the group of Jesus' disciples, who must have listened astounded to these words. Around Jesus, now, true prayer – the prayer that any may pray, from any nation – is offered. *He* is now the place of prayer.

5 Who's behind it?

Mark 11:27–33

Back into Jerusalem – and again straight to the temple, where Jesus is confronted by a delegation from the Sanhedrin, the Jewish ruling council. We are reminded of the earlier delegation from Jerusalem which came to Galilee to investigate Jesus, and of their conclusion: 'He has Beelzebul, and casts out demons by the prince of demons!' (3:22). There the issue was the same, as here – whose authority is at work? The suspicion of these Jewish leaders, following Jesus' violent action the previous day, is that he is acting by Satanic authority in attacking the temple in this way. They want a confession.

In good Jewish debating style, Jesus answers with a counter-question (vv. 29–30). Why does he ask this particular question about John the Baptist? It might be because Jesus' authority as Son of God derives from that marvellous descent of the dove at his baptism by John, and the heavenly voice that accompanied the gift of the Spirit (1:9–11). Or it might be because the whole focus of John's ministry was to call attention to 'one stronger than I, coming after me, the lace of whose sandals I am not worthy to bend and untie!' (1:7). If the Jerusalem authorities really believed in John as a prophet, they would have been watching for the coming of this 'stronger one' and might be open to seeing Jesus as that figure.

There is truth in both these thoughts, I think, but actually they miss the heart of the matter. Jesus asks not about John, but specifically about his *baptism*: 'John's baptism – was it of divine or human origin?' (v. 30). The point is that John's baptism was 'a baptism of repentance for the forgiveness of sins' (1:4) – in other words, John, too, offered forgiveness of sins apart from the Jerusalem cult and temple, just as Jesus does here in verse 25. John sidelined the temple by offering people a glorious experience of cleansing direct from God himself, as they stepped into the Jordan and heard his prophetic declaration of forgiveness as the water sluiced over them. Again, no need for doves or lambs.

Was that of God? These temple aficionados are not ready to agree with that. But they know they are out of step with popular opinion about John. So… Jesus' question skilfully exposes their fixed determination *not* to accept that he was acting under God's authority when he overturned those tables.

6 No fruit

Verse 12 oozes with irony. The very telling of this parable creates a reaction which proves its truth! The temple authorities obligingly cast themselves as the tenant farmers who want to get rid of the Son – and do so with their eyes open: 'They realised that he had spoken the parable against them.'

'God's vineyard' was a frequently used metaphor for Israel, and there is a particularly important passage in Isaiah 5 which undoubtedly lies behind Jesus' use of the image here. In Isaiah, too, God looks for fruit from his carefully tended vineyard but receives none – and so declares that he will dig the vineyard up and destroy its walls (Isaiah 5:5–6). In Jesus' retelling it is the wicked tenants who are to be destroyed, not the vineyard itself (v. 9). Actually, the vineyard is to get a make-over – a new cornerstone, a restoration planned and executed by God himself which 'is wonderful in our eyes' (v. 11).

And that brings us to the even bigger irony at the heart of this parable: it is the *rejection* of the stone by the builders which is the key event. When they kill the Son and throw him out of the vineyard, trying to claim it for themselves, the tenants start a process which leads not just to their own destruction but also to the rebuilding of the vineyard, with new tenants as well as a new 'cornerstone'. This is Jesus' judgement on the temple authorities. They claim the temple for their own, but precisely through their rejection of Jesus and his word God will bring the temple to its true destiny – there will be a house of prayer for all nations!

We must not miss the note of dreadful suffering at the heart of this parable. One by one the messengers are rejected, beaten and killed. And then the owner's 'beloved Son' – who had every right, as the heir, to enforce the terms of the tenancy – is also brutally murdered. There is no way round the awfulness of this and the folly. The cross is looming. The madness will triumph. God's people will assert their own power and will murder God's Son and God's spokespersons. But through that suffering God brings a restoration 'wonderful in our eyes'. It is ever so! The suffering of God's true people is never in vain – that's the message. Always it leads to wonderful new growth and fruitfulness, through the pain.

Guidelines

We seem to have travelled a long way in one week! What has particularly stood out for you in our readings this week?

For me, it has been the horrifying way in which religion can gain a life of its own and end up opposing God's purposes and plan in the world: the fruitless temple, symbolised by the barren and dying fig tree, failing in its calling to be a house of prayer for all nations because it has become a place of exclusion; the fruitless vineyard (fruitless for its owner), symbolising Israel's captivity to an elite who want to bolster their own power and not submit to God's word.

Where do I sit with that – where am I? Am I ready to sacrifice my own plans and status when God says 'Stop!' to something I love? Am I ready to give up my ambitions and submit to his? Am I ready to rethink deeply held convictions, if God's Spirit seems to be requiring this?

The positive side of this is the beautiful picture of prayer around Jesus Christ in 11:22–25. He is the new 'place' of prayer, of *expansive* prayer, prayer for which nothing is impossible – no mountain too great that it cannot be moved. 'Have faith in God!' he says (11:22). Have I – have we – begun truly to have that kind of faith? A faith that can *imagine* grandly, that can imagine a whole landscape being remodelled by God's loving and creative power (11:23)? What landscapes might God be wanting to redesign around you?

1 Taxes or not?

Mark 12:13-17

'They sent to him…' (v. 13) sets the scene for the rest of chapter 12, where we spend this week. 'They' are the Sanhedrin, the Jewish authorities with whom Jesus has been in dialogue since 11:27 – and who will ultimately be responsible for his death (14:1, 55). They now send him representatives of the various groups within the Sanhedrin in turn, to examine him: the Pharisees today, next the Sadducees (12:18–27), and finally the 'scribes' (12:28–34). A theme throughout, as we might expect, is the interpretation of scripture.

Scripture underlies today's famous exchange with the Pharisees and Herodians, about tax. They want to force Jesus into a trap (v. 13) by making him take sides in a hotly argued theological and practical problem: should God's chosen people, owing allegiance only to God as King and Lord, implicitly recognise the authority of Rome by agreeing to the Romans' tax demands? If Jesus says 'No' to this, he will incur the wrath of Rome (and the disapproval of the Herodians). If he says 'Yes', he will incur the wrath of the Zealot separatists. But either way, he will be agreeing with the presupposition behind the whole dispute, namely that Israel is fundamentally distinct, made different by election and by possession of the law and the temple. As we've already seen, Jesus sets a question mark against this by his treatment of the temple (11:16–17), just as earlier he set a question mark against it by 'declaring all foods clean' (7:19), abolishing one of Israel's fundamental distinctives.

His very clever answer here (v. 17) heads in the same direction. The 'denarius' (v. 15) was a Roman coin bearing the image of the emperor Tiberius, widely used in Israelite commerce and also to pay the Roman poll tax. The very fact that his opponents possess such coins in their pockets show that they are deeply involved in Caesar's world already. They are part of it – how can they not be? But whose world is it, in fact? 'The earth is the Lord's and all that is in it, the world, and those who live in it' (Psalm 24:1, NRSV). And 'those who live in it' – of whatever nation – bear the image of the God who made them, just as those coins bear Tiberius' image. How can we deal faithfully in *that* coinage – the currency that is all human life, indeed all creation, belonging to God?

2 You are seriously mistaken!

The Sadducees were the Jewish aristocrats – the wealthy leading families from whom the high priests were drawn. They defined themselves not just economically and socially but also theologically, because they accepted as scripture only the five books of the Torah (Genesis to Deuteronomy) and on that basis rejected the Pharisees' strong belief in the resurrection. The final resurrection is barely taught in the Old Testament (see, for example, Daniel 12:2), and nowhere in the Torah, but by the first century it had become a widespread belief not only among Pharisees – see Martha's confession of it in John 11:23–24.

The Sadducees' silly story, based on the practice of levirate marriage (vv. 19–23), is meant to explode the whole idea of resurrection by making it produce a ridiculous state of affairs. Once again, Jesus agrees with neither side in this debate. He does not agree with the Pharisees' view of the resurrection, for they believed in the continuation of marriage and sex in God's resurrected kingdom. Nor does he agree with the Sadducees' denial of the whole idea. He speaks entirely with his own authority, both about God and about the scriptures: 'Isn't this why you are mistaken – you know neither the Scriptures nor the power of God!' (v. 24)

God's power produces a whole new kind of human being and human relating after resurrection (v. 25): what will that be like? And the notion of resurrection is well founded in the Torah, Jesus insists, quoting Exodus 3:6 (v. 26). It is not immediately clear how this verse teaches resurrection – until we realise that Exodus 3:6 expresses the basic covenant commitment that underlay Israel's whole relationship with God. God has *committed* himself to Abraham, Isaac and Jacob (and their descendants), and it is unimaginable that their death will change that commitment. So the dead are still the objects of God's covenant love, and therefore still in intimate connection with him, and belief in resurrection follows! This seems to be the shape of Jesus' scriptural argument in verses 26–27.

This is the scriptural basis of belief in life after death: it rests not on some power within us, an immortal 'bit' (a soul) which lives on, but wholly on the power of God who brings us to resurrection because he is committed to us in Christ. Our relationship with him is what survives death – see how beautifully Paul expresses this in Romans 14:7–9.

3 The greatest commandment

Now Jesus engages with a representative of the third Sanhedrin grouping – a single scribe who has been impressed by his reply to the Sadducees. The question he asks, 'What is the first commandment, the most important of all?' (v. 28) was frequently debated by the rabbis. Jesus is ready with his reply, which combines two commandments, in fact – the so-called 'Shema' from Deuteronomy 6:4–5 (the command to 'love the Lord your God') and Leviticus 19:18, the command to 'love your neighbour as yourself'.

Jews were very familiar with the Shema, which they were supposed to recite every morning and evening. 'Shema' means 'hear', the first word of the text Jesus quotes – and it has extra significance here because this scribe has been doing it: 'One of the scribes approached him. He had *heard* the debate, and had seen how well Jesus responded' (v. 28). This scribe has been truly listening!

So undoubtedly he will also notice how Jesus changes the Shema here. Jesus adds a fourth 'all': to 'heart,' 'soul' and 'strength' drawn from Deuteronomy, he adds 'mind' in the middle. The scribe does not object, but when he responds in verse 33 he quotes Deuteronomy correctly, without the addition of 'mind'. He clearly thinks that Jesus is right to choose these two verses as the greatest in the law (v. 32), and adds his own comment: these two commands 'are much more important than all burnt offerings and sacrifices' (v. 33b). They are standing in the temple as he says this – the place whose whole raison d'être was the proper performance of burnt offerings and sacrifices! This scribe truly has been listening – not just to Jesus' debate with the Sadducees, but also to his attack on the temple regime as undermining God's plan that it should be a house of prayer for all, Gentiles included (11:15–17).

And that brings us back to Jesus' addition to the Shema. 'When Jesus saw that he replied *mindfully* he said to him, "You are not far from the kingdom of God"' (v. 34). The word I have translated 'mindfully' comes from the same Greek root as the word 'mind' in verse 30 – the fourth 'all' with which he tells us to love God. This scribe is doing it – loving God *thoughtfully*, which means beginning to see Jesus as holding a dangerous, exciting new authority alongside the law, and being ready to break moulds and think the unthinkable!

4 'The son of David'?

Many English translations swallow up a vital word at the start of verse 35: 'In reply, Jesus said as he taught in the temple.' 'In reply' disappears in the standard translations (e.g. NRSV and NIV), but it is important in marking a transition here. Having seen off the attacks from the three Sanhedrin groups in verses 13–34 (three paragraphs), we now have three paragraphs in which Jesus 'replies', i.e. he goes on the offensive, first in public (paragraphs 1 and 2, vv. 35–40) and then in private (paragraph 3, vv. 41–44).

These three responses take forward the challenge to think differently which Jesus has just issued – namely that we cannot properly love God unless our *minds* are engaged, so that we are ready to resist old polarities (God or Caesar) and read the scriptures from new angles (the covenant relationship entails resurrection!). We need truly to *listen* with fresh ears because the new is afoot – and this is always so for the church of Jesus Christ. The challenge of the new never goes away.

This first 'reply' concerns a new reading of a very familiar text. Psalm 110 (v. 36) was originally a coronation hymn, celebrating the symbolic installation of Israel's new Davidic king at God's right hand. But in the first century it was widely read as messianic, that is, as referring to the coming king who will rule over Israel's enemies. So it fits closely with Mark's kingdom theme, and in particular relates to that Palm Sunday cry, 'Blessed is the coming kingdom of our father David!' (11:10). 'Son of David' was a widely used title for the Messiah, as we saw with Bartimaeus in 10:47–48.

So *think!* says Jesus: if David is the author of this psalm (as all would accept – no one questioned the truth of the ascription to David at the head of the psalm), then David is addressing the Messiah as his 'Lord', not his 'son'. Sons simply follow in their father's footsteps, so if the Messiah is David's 'son', then the kingdom will look much the same. But if he is David's 'Lord', then all bets are off. Anything is possible. The kingdom can be completely recast under a wholly new authority over which David has no veto. And who become the enemies over whom this 'Lord' will be victorious? Not necessarily Rome, but all who resist his rule.

5 The last word

With this little paragraph Jesus' public ministry in Mark's gospel ends, although he has plenty yet to say about Israel's public figures and institutions. 'The huge crowd was hearing him with delight,' Mark tells us (v. 37b) – they too are truly 'hearing' as the Shema requires (v. 29) – but we can imagine that some of them would have been shocked by what follows: a full-on attack on pretentious and rapacious scribes who flaunt their position and wealth.

'Watch out for the scribes who like walking around in long prayer-robes and being greeted in the marketplaces, who seek the platform seats in the synagogues and the head of the table at banquets! They devour the houses of widows and show off with long prayers. They will receive overflowing judgement!' (vv. 38–40). We must not overread this – Jesus is not attacking *all* scribes, but 'the scribes who…' We can certainly imagine that the scribe of verse 34, and all like him, are not included here. But people gave instinctive respect to all scribes, the teachers of the law who were also leaders of the community – rising to let them pass in the marketplaces, giving them high honour in the synagogues and on all festive occasions, and believing without question – as the scribes themselves did – that their wealth was clear evidence of the blessing of God, a reward for their righteousness.

Nonsense, says Jesus. The wealth of some of these scribes rests on extortion and the exploitation of the poor (v. 40). He does not mince his words. In this case, new thinking entails a radical social critique which is ready to expose corruption and injustice, even in the most unexpected places. Far from evidencing God's blessing, their wealth is going to bring them into 'overwhelming judgement' – a very strong expression (v. 40) which implies that they, more than all, will fall under God's judgement.

It is a sobering note on which to end Jesus' public ministry. Just as he began this period of his Jerusalem ministry by attacking the temple (11:15–18), so now he ends it by attacking the scribes who were the pillars of the temple establishment and who, with the chief priests, responded to his temple action by 'seeking how to kill him' (11:18). It's all about his authority – in this case, authority to specify the direction of God's judgement and to expose the injustice which God will condemn.

6 The greatest giver

Jesus is still in the temple – in the Court of the Women, in fact, where the treasury was. Gentiles were not allowed into this court, and women could not go beyond it, into the Court of Israel, where only men could enter. Jesus is so struck by what he sees as he watches the activity around the treasury that he calls his disciples together to speak to them.

Why does Mark include this beautiful story here? It has a very prominent place in his narrative, right at the end of Jesus' public ministry, and it in effect introduces the great apocalyptic discourse that follows in chapter 13, which is a continuation of the same private chat with his disciples.

This desperately poor widow, giving all that she has to the temple, is at the opposite end of the scale to the wealthy scribes Jesus was just talking about (vv. 38–40). But the point is not just the contrast between them. There are two vital things to notice here – first that she is *seen* and second that she is *judged*. Nobody else noticed her tiny presence, and her tiny gift, in the swirling crowd of high-class donors pressing around the treasury. But Jesus noticed her. Nothing escapes his attention, Mark is telling us.

And he doesn't just see. Judgement is the theme that unites this story with what precedes – and indeed with what follows. Judgement in the Bible never loses its flavour of being the King's verdict: the King speaks the final truth to which all must submit, gives the story its final definitive shape and tells it how it really is, behind all appearances. When the verdict is negative, 'judgement' becomes equivalent to 'condemnation'. And here is the King's verdict: those highly respected scribes will receive 'overwhelming judgement' (v. 40 – i.e. condemnation) for their self-promotion and hidden oppression of people like this widow, while she will be celebrated as the giver of the greatest gift – far more than the rich around her, in fact, 'her whole life' (v. 44). She models the self-giving of the Son of Man himself (see 10:45).

Jesus' judgement here completely reverses the scale of values that society then lived by – which saw wealth as a sign of God's approval and poverty as the opposite. We realise again how much the kingdom cuts across the 'normal' registers of value, so that 'many who are first will be last, and the last first' (10:31).

Guidelines

We cannot be authentic followers of Jesus Christ today if we do not take on board the enormous challenge of the reversal of values which we met in the last two readings this week. This is nothing new in Mark – we have met it before. Indeed, the parallel story, which leads into the section of Jesus' public Jerusalem ministry which ends here, focused on a similar figure – blind Bartimaeus, penniless and powerless, rejected by the crowd around Jesus, but seen and privileged by him (10:46–52).

As you reflect on this, what implications do you see for:

- the way churches are led and organised?
- relations between western and 'developing world' churches?
- Christian social action and mission?
- giving and fundraising in churches?
- your own local church?
- your own life as a Christian?

The uniting theme this week is the new thinking that arises from and around Jesus as an authority who critiques the law and all our customary ways of seeing things and acting in the world. The kingdom brings a new scale of values, along with new ways of reading scripture – and we will love God with our minds as we think these through and seek to be fresh in our faithfulness to *him*, rather than solely to the traditions that have shaped us. This is a huge challenge! Life throws new things at us regularly, anyway, and we have to respond with creativity, with love and with the values of the kingdom.

In what ways do you think that Christ might be calling you to be fresh in your faithfulness to him?

1 Magnificent, but doomed

Mark 13:1–4

The Jerusalem temple was a truly magnificent structure – built with enormous stones (still visible in the so-called 'Wailing Wall', which is all that now remains) and overlaid with gold on the side facing the Mount of Olives, where Jesus sits to rest. Here, four disciples approach him with an astonished question in response to his prediction that 'not one of these stones will be left upon another – all will be thrown down' (v. 2).

Their question shows how seriously they take him as a prophet: 'Tell us, when will this be? And what sign will indicate that all this is about to be fulfilled?' (v. 4). They know his words were not a throwaway comment about impermanence, but a specific prophecy of destruction. And in response we have one of the most striking chapters in the gospels, indeed in the New Testament. We will spend this week reading and thinking about it. It is the longest connected piece of teaching from Jesus in Mark, and it takes us into the mysterious and intriguing world of apocalyptic.

There are versions of this chapter in all three synoptic gospels. Matthew's wording of the disciples' question is interestingly different from Mark's: 'Tell us, when will this be? And what will be the sign of your coming and of the fulfilment of the age?' (Matthew 24:3). The centrepiece of the chapter is a beautifully evocative description of 'the coming of the Son of Man' (Mark 13:24–27), so Jesus' response to the disciples seems to grow beyond the destruction of the temple – and Matthew reflects this in the introductory question. But Mark does not, and so raises for us the question of how Jesus' answer addresses the disciples' question, and whether it goes beyond it – and if so, why.

Apocalyptic is all about 'seeing' things differently, with new eyes. Jesus' answer carries on the process of new 'seeing' which underlies the radical upside-down view of the scribes and of the widow in 12:38–44 and broadens this out. The exchange that starts it all in verses 1–2 introduces two different verbs for seeing, which become the structural key for the chapter: 'See [*horan*] – what magnificent stones and buildings!' says the unnamed disciple. 'Do you see [*blepein*] these great buildings?' replies Jesus. Tomorrow we will explore how these two verbs set the scene for the new seeing which this powerful apocalyptic discourse will give us.

2 Watch out!

A bit more about our two verbs (see yesterday): *blepein* means 'see – and watch out! Take care!'; *horan* has a more general meaning, 'see and notice' – in apocalyptic use, it's usually about seeing something of special significance or great import.

Our chapter has six paragraphs, three introduced by *blepein* (numbers 1, 2 and 6) and three by *horan* (numbers 3, 4 and 5; though in two cases *horan* is a significant word within the paragraph, rather than the introductory word, as we will see). So we have three calls to 'watch out' surrounding three significant apocalyptic 'seeings' or appearances. Today's reading contains the first two paragraphs; we will look at the remaining four on successive days this week.

First, Jesus tells his disciples to 'watch out' so as not to be deceived by false messiahs (vv. 5–6) and not to be upset by wars, conflict and turmoil in the world around them (vv. 7–8). 'Such things must be,' he says, 'but the End is not yet!' (v. 7). Second, he tells them to 'watch out for yourselves' (v. 9), because they are going to experience persecution from the world (vv. 9–11) and opposition from their families (vv. 12–13) – in fact, 'you will be hated by all because of my name: but the one who endures to the End will be saved!' (v. 13).

These two references to 'the End' make us wonder how Jesus is addressing the shocked question posed by Peter, James, John and Andrew. They did not ask about 'the End', but about his terrible prediction of temple destruction. However, we must remember the central role given to the temple in God's plan for Israel and for the world – it was meant to be 'the house of prayer for all nations' (11:17). So if God is going to knock it down, what will happen to this vital aim of uniting the world in worship? As we'll see, something even more amazing is afoot.

But they did ask about 'signs' – 'what will be the sign that all this is about to be fulfilled?' (v. 4). 'Birth pangs' are signs of something wonderful about to happen, and Jesus is teaching them (and us) to see wars, conflict, distress, persecution and family betrayal not *just* as awful things to be endured but also as signs of the coming End – and of an imminent End, too, like birth pangs before the birth: signs of coming salvation (v. 13) and not just disasters to be borne.

3 The sacrilege that causes abandonment

'But when you see…' (v. 14): the 'but' and the change in the verb for 'seeing' (*horan*) show that we are moving from the signs to the thing signified. Something appropriately called 'the desolating sacrilege' will appear, in response to which Jesus' followers in Judea must 'flee to the mountains', because an absolutely terrible time of suffering is about to begin, described in horrifying language in verses 15–20. In response to this suffering, many 'false Christs and false prophets' will also appear, but the disciples must 'watch out' (*blepein*, v. 23), so as not to be deceived by them.

The expression 'desolating sacrilege' comes from Daniel 11:31 and 12:11 (also in 1 Maccabees 1:54), where it refers to the events of 167BC when the Syrian king Antiochus Epiphanes took over the Jerusalem temple, abolished the sacrifices and the worship of the God of Israel and set up an altar to himself as Zeus. This prior fulfilment lies behind Mark's beautifully enigmatic comment 'let the reader understand' (v. 14), because clearly – prompted by Jesus' prophecy – he expects it to appear again and invites his readers to judge whether what they are seeing constitutes 'the desolating sacrilege' or not. Apocalyptic always works like this – it puts us, as readers and interpreters, on the spot to decide what constitutes a fulfilment of the vision.

There was certainly a fulfilment in the Jewish war of AD67–73. Zealot factions turned the temple into a military base, which was then besieged, stormed and destroyed by Roman forces in AD70, with terrible suffering for the local people. Thousands died. When all this was looming, the Christians in Jerusalem left, in obedience to Jesus' warning, and fled across the Jordan to a place called Pella.

The question for us is: does this obvious reference and fulfilment of the prophecy exhaust its significance? Are the warning birth pangs (vv. 5–13) just meant for the period leading up to AD70? The fact that this is a reapplication of Daniel's 'desolating sacrilege' prophecy allows us as readers – let the reader understand! – to interpret our 'times' in the same way: we too can see war, conflict and societal disruption not just as the dreadful disasters they are, but also as signs of coming salvation – because God is the same God, and the Son of Man will come just when sacrilege and desolation are at their worst… but that is to anticipate tomorrow's passage!

4 'And then they will see the Son of Man'

We've reached the climax! This is the point where the listening disciples, and Mark's first readers, expect Jesus to say, 'And then the temple will be destroyed.' But he doesn't – he seems to have left that focus behind. Or has he? Actually those first hearers and readers, knowing what apocalyptic does, would hear the destruction of the temple in the 'cosmic collapse' language in verses 24–25. So significant an event is it in the *spiritual* structure of the world that the destruction of the temple is like the stars falling from the skies. Peter, quoting Joel, uses similar language about Pentecost in Acts 2:19–20.

And because it is apocalyptic, the focus can fall elsewhere, so that our sight is directed beyond the disaster to God's plan and action. When all is collapsing – when that terrible event occurs that overturns the universe for Israel's sense of her place in God's plan – 'then they will see the Son of Man coming in the clouds with great power and glory. And then he will send the angels, and will gather his elect from the four winds, from the furthest corners of earth and heaven' (vv. 26–27). The moment of destruction will be the moment of salvation!

'They will see' is significant – this is not just a private vision for the disciples (contrast 'you' in verse 14), but a public revelation. And as in the Daniel 7 vision which lies behind Jesus' words here (especially Daniel 7:13–14), this is about 'the Son of Man' displacing the power of all earthly kingdoms and coming to set up his own kingdom on earth – a universal kingdom in which 'the elect' from all nations are gathered in and united around his throne in love, peace and healing (v. 27). Jesus the Son of Man will fulfil the role of the temple to be the place where all nations meet God at last (11:17)!

Belief in the second coming of Jesus Christ – to set up his kingdom on earth – is absolutely basic to New Testament faith. But there's no doubt: Jesus' first hearers would certainly have heard him say that the Son of Man will come when the temple is destroyed. Paul believed that too, it seems – see 2 Thessalonians 2:4–8. But the destruction occurred in AD70, and the Son of Man did not come. How are we to understand this? We will tackle this difficult question tomorrow.

5 Summer is near

There is a strange tension in these verses. First the little fig tree parable (v. 28) picks up the idea of 'signs that point ahead' from the disciples' question in verse 4 and Jesus' reply in verses 5–23. Picking up his encouragement to 'watch out – I have told you all this in advance!' (v. 23), the parable pictures seeing the signs of summer in the fig's bursting new leaves. 'So also you: when you see [*horan*] these things happening, know that he is near, standing at the gates!' (v. 29). And this whole sequence – both the signs and the events signified – will occur within 'this generation' (v. 30), secured on the unshakeable authority of Jesus Christ whose words are more sure and lasting than the universe itself (v. 31).

So why then verse 32? 'But concerning that day and hour no one knows – neither the angels in heaven, nor even the Son: only the Father knows.' As illustrated by the next little parable (vv. 33–37), his coming *cannot* be predicted by signs foreshadowing: 'You do not know when the moment will arrive!' (v. 33).

In fact verse 32 was very helpful when Christians puzzled over the non-appearance of the Son of Man in response to the terrible events of AD70. The Romans overran Jerusalem and the temple amid appalling carnage and suffering, but the promised overthrow of all earthly kingdoms by the Son of Man coming in power and glory, and the gathering of the nations – where were they? Christians realised that 'all these things' in verse 30 refers to the signs, the 'desolating sacrilege' and the final crushing of Jerusalem, *and not to the coming of Christ*. That still remains as a hope for all who suffer and long for deliverance.

On this basis, the terrible 'signs' described so powerfully in verses 5–23 are liberated from restriction to the first century. *Wherever* war, conflict, famine, disease, persecution and social turmoil blight our societies – indeed, wherever some especially dreadful 'desolating sacrilege' seems to threaten all goodness, humanity and hope – then we can be confident that Jesus is 'at the gates' (v. 29), because he is never far from those who suffer. He comes to overthrow the rule of evil: he comes when we pray and cast ourselves on his mercy – and one day he will come 'in the clouds' and transform all things by his just and merciful rule.

6 Keep your eyes peeled!

Mark 13:33–37

The chapter ends with another little parable, this time underlining the complete unpredictability of Jesus' coming – in response to which, Jesus says, we must not 'shelve' the whole idea of his return ('sleep', v. 36), but be ready for his coming at any moment.

So there are two traps to be avoided – on the one hand, trying to give a date to the second coming and, on the other, ignoring the second coming completely as a feature of Christian faith and hope. In different places and ways, the Christian church has been guilty of both. Jesus uses three verbs to underline his appeal ('watch out', 'be alert', 'stay awake' – one of these in every verse except 36), and he widens it out to include all readers of Mark: 'What I say to you I say to all: stay awake!' (v. 37).

Interestingly, the parable does not encourage a passive otherworldliness. This would be a third trap, into which we know that some early Christians fell. They gave up work in order simply to wait for Christ's return (see 2 Thessalonians 3:6–13). Here, Jesus is clear that the 'slaves' left behind must prepare for their master's return by performing the 'work' that he has given them (v. 34).

If we asked, 'What 'work' is that?', we would notice that Mark 13 gives a particular answer to this question, an answer which also gives a further perspective on the non-appearance of the Son of Man in AD70. Why did he not come then? This must have been a teasing question for Christians reading this 'apocalyptic discourse' in the latter part of the first century. But they will surely have noticed the subtle answer which the chapter provides – and which at the same time fills out the nature of the 'job' left to do. In 13:9–10 Jesus gives his disciples a terrifying task – in spite of opposition, to 'stand before governors and kings, for my sake, to bear witness to them. First the gospel must be proclaimed to all nations!' Here 'first' means 'before the End comes' (see verse 7). The Son of Man did not come in AD70, because this prior condition had not yet been fulfilled – and at the same time, here are the marching orders, the 'work' for the servants to do on behalf of their master, before he comes again. A task still unfulfilled. What does it mean to 'preach the gospel to all the nations'?

Guidelines

What a rich feast this chapter is. What do you think about this kind of apocalyptic writing? It can be deeply puzzling and alienating, not least because it seems to portray a God who inflicts wars and distress on the world for no apparent reason. 'Such things must be,' says Jesus (13:7) – but why? If God is God, then he lies behind that 'must'. Can he not run his world without inflicting such horrors on humanity?

This is the rich theological soil in which apocalyptic flourishes. Jesus is actually echoing Daniel in these words – see Daniel 2:28, 45, where Daniel is foreseeing the rise and fall of kingdoms and the eventual overthrow of all earthly rule and power by the kingdom of God. In Daniel earthly power is given by God to earthly rulers, who may abuse their power and become 'bestial' – and the 'beasts' are the powerful symbols of terrifying secular power displaced by the Son of Man when he receives the kingdom in Daniel 7. God doesn't *create* the beasts in Daniel, but (a) he appeals to earthly rulers to do good, (b) he limits their power to do evil and (c) he finally steps in to remove them and establish his own 'direct rule'.

We meet all these ideas in Mark 13, where – as we have seen – the Daniel Son of Man vision is the glorious centrepiece of the chapter. This is political theology, in which the kingdom of God is not an otherworldly reality but our hope for deliverance from the dreadful rule of oppressive earthly powers – like Rome. And while we 'watch out', longing to 'see' that Day, the task is to 'preach the gospel to all nations' (13:10), because that is the power which even now can transform the governors and kings to whom it is proclaimed (13:9). Christ will not come again, until that great task has been achieved!

FURTHER READING

James R. Edwards, *The Gospel according to Mark* (Eerdmans/Apollos, 2002).

Stephen Motyer, *Come Lord Jesus! A biblical theology of the second coming of Christ* (Apollos, 2016): chapter 4 is on Mark 13.

Tom Wright, *Mark for Everyone* (SPCK, 2001).

Revelation 1—11: drawing back the curtain

Stephen Finamore

Recent research into the book of Revelation draws our attention to the group of people that John calls 'my brothers the prophets'. Some writers think that the author shared his visions and his understanding of them with these colleagues and that when he had written them down in a book, they took responsibility for going around the churches, reading out the text and helping the churches to interpret it. This set of studies imagines that we are present to hear John introduce the final version of his book to his fellow prophets, to instruct them on its meaning and to send them out to the churches to teach the contents.

Unless otherwise stated, Bible quotations are taken from the NRSV.

A message from John

Lots of you will know this already, but it won't hurt you to be reminded. Others of you are new and you need to hear this because it forms the foundation for everything else. Here are the seven – appropriately! – keys to understanding and teaching the book. Keep these in mind and you will serve the churches well.

1. Jesus gave me an *apocalypse*. This means an unveiling or a revelation. The visions are intended to show things that are currently hidden, in whole or in part, from us and from the world of our day. Your job is to pull back the curtain so that the churches see things as they truly are. You will show them the hidden spiritual realities that are at work in the world.

2. Most of the action takes place in – or is seen from the standpoint of – heaven; and heaven is God's temple. This temple used to have an earthly counterpart, or shadow, in Jerusalem. Like the one in Jerusalem, the heavenly true temple has, among other things, a Holy Place and a Holy of Holies. The heavenly Holy of Holies is God's true dwelling place.

3. The book of Revelation tells you – in a new way – a story you already know. The apostles tell us that Messiah Jesus died for our sins, that he ascended into the presence of God in heaven, that the message about him is to be proclaimed

throughout the world and that he will return in glory as king and judge. The visions of the book express these things and their consequences.

4. The book does not necessarily go in chronological order. It goes in the order in which I received the visions. At points, it celebrates the end of all things and then goes back to tell the story again from another perspective. It all happens from the point of view of heaven and – you might have guessed it – time works differently there. I suppose that's a good definition of prophecy – to tell people how things are from heaven's perspective.

5. The book is an account of the visions that I received *and* the fruit of my reflection on those visions. I have written it so that it rewards careful reflection and study. You will see that certain numbers are especially important. We will discuss them as we go.

6. I am not aware of many direct quotations of the Hebrew scriptures in the book. However, it is full of allusions to the Bible. In particular, it would be a good idea to be familiar with the books of Exodus, Psalms, Isaiah, Ezekiel, Daniel and Zechariah. Many of the people in the churches will not know their Bibles well. Part of your job is to help them see how this Revelation fits in with God's previous revelation and forms its climax.

7. The visons tell of things that will happen soon. They've already begun. The task is urgent. The persecution of which Messiah Jesus spoke is already upon us. The book reminds us that the victory over the forces of evil is already won. We now need to remain true to Jesus, persevering in our loyalty to him whatever may be thrown at us – or to whatever we may be thrown!

1 It begins

Revelation 1

This is the unveiling of the true state of the world, and it belongs to Messiah Jesus. He received it from God and gave it to me through an angel. I now pass it on to you to give to God's people. When you do, both you and they will be blessed.

The book is a letter sent in the name of God, the Spirit and Messiah Jesus. The number seven suggests completeness. The seven churches therefore represent the whole church. The seven spirits are the fullness of the Holy Spirit of God.

The whole is dedicated to Jesus, who has saved us for a purpose and who will come again. And it's all about God, who is the one who bookends everything.

As you know, it all started when the persecution took me to Patmos. I was in prayer one Sunday when a voice told me to write to the churches. When I turned to look, I found I was in heaven and stood in the Holy Place gazing at the Menorah. There in the middle of it was Jesus dressed as a high priest, except he had no turban, and so I could see his hair was like God's in Daniel's vision. His weapon was the word that he speaks, and his face shone like that of Moses after he'd been in God's presence.

I knew this was the true Day of Atonement, and our high priest had come from the Holy of Holies, where he had made atonement for the sins of the world. We can read about this in the letter written to our persecuted brothers and sisters (Hebrews). Of course, I fell in wonder and worship. And then he told me a great mystery. Our churches do not belong to earth alone. They also belong in heaven. Just as the temple had its heavenly counterpart, so do the churches. Their heavenly presence is held safe in the right hand of Jesus and he walks among them.

2 The letters

Revelation 2—3

There are seven letters, and the number seven indicates that, in addition to being for their specific recipients right now, they are for the whole church today and always. As you know, seven is the number of completeness and the number of God.

Most of the letters follow a structure with seven points in it. First, each is addressed to the church's angel. This is a reference back to the opening vision, when I saw the ascended Jesus with seven stars in his hands and learned that these were the church's angels. I believe that these are a dimension of the churches that is already a part of heaven. Next, there is a description of Jesus that draws on an aspect of the opening vision. Then there is something for which the church is praised, and fourthly there is some criticism. After that the church gets some instructions as to what it should now do. The sixth element is a call to pay attention, and each letter ends with a promise to the ones who conquer. These are the ones who stay faithful to Jesus even under the threat of death.

As you study the letters, you will see that some of them do not quite follow this pattern. Jesus may have seen nothing worth praising in one church and another may have warranted only encouragement. If you spot where the pattern is broken, you will see that silence can speak volumes.

3 The vision of an expectant heaven

Revelation 4

After the seventh letter I looked around the heavenly version of the Holy Place and saw an open door. I knew that in the earthly temple a veil used to hang between the Holy Place and the Holy of Holies and that at the death of Jesus it had torn in two. The same voice that told me to write now summoned me into the Holy of Holies, the dwelling place of God. As you would expect, I saw God's throne. Circled round the throne are elders who are responsible for the worship of heaven; they are the heavenly counterparts of the 24 courses of priests that we know about from Chronicles. All the signs of God's covenant making are present: the rainbow from Genesis and thunder and lightning from Sinai. All this suggests that God is longing to keep his ancient covenant promises.

The throne is made of the four living beings who sing to God just like the seraphs in Isaiah's vision. Then I understood that soon the elders would be handing over their responsibilities. The elders will throw down their crowns because they will relinquish their authority for carrying out atonement. It will no longer be a task of the earthly temple and so there'll be something new in heaven as well. I've carefully put the key verbs in the future tense, but I've got a horrible feeling someone will try to pretend they are present continuous. This will unhelpfully imply that the vision is of heaven as it is in eternity, rather than when it is expecting a radical change. In fact, all heaven seemed to be on tiptoe waiting to see what God would do.

4 Heaven welcomes the exalted Messiah

Revelation 5

We are all used to hearing the story of how Jesus ascended into heaven. We tell it from the perspective of those on earth. In this vision we see it from the point of view of those waiting for the Messiah in heaven. Only when he arrives can the scroll containing the promises of God be opened so that the process of fulfilment can begin. As soon as I saw the scroll, I knew what it was. All of heaven was waiting, longing for the day when the scroll would be opened. Imagine my distress when it looked like it would stay sealed.

Then I heard of one who could open it. In these visions, I sometimes *hear* something in the language of what was promised in the ancient prophecies. And so, I was told about a great warrior, the Lion of Judah. Of course, when I looked – and *seeing* is the language of the way God has chosen to fulfil his promises – I saw, in the middle of the creatures who make up the throne of God, a sacrificed Lamb, who was clearly Messiah Jesus. He had conquered, had been faithful even to the point of death, and so he could take the scroll and bring God's promises to fulfilment.

At this point some of the things anticipated earlier actually happened, for example, the elders fell before the throne. The prayers of earth were answered, and so heaven sang a new song. It's a song about the work of atonement accomplished by the Lamb. Now God's forgiveness is not for Israel alone, but the promise to Abraham is fulfilled and people from every nation are part of the people of God.

The next thing I knew was that the whole of creation was praising God – the whole earth was filled with his glory. I realised I was being given a taste of the end and the renewal of all things. In Messiah Jesus, God had already done all that needed to be done to fulfil his promises. Heaven could rejoice. In the next vision I would see how all this would play out on earth. In one sense the end had come, but in another sense the end was just beginning.

5 The end begins

Revelation 6:1–8

The Messiah opened the first seal on the scroll and the process of the fulfilment of God's promises began. At the time, I wondered, 'What would be the first effect of Jesus' exaltation in heaven?' If you think about it, you already know the answer. The living creature like a lion called out, 'Go,' and out went a rider with a crown on a white horse. The clue to the riders' identities is in what they do. This one goes out conquering and to conquer – and we have already seen that this is what Messiah Jesus did and what his churches are required to do. We are sent out, empowered by the Holy Spirit, to proclaim the gospel, to witness to Jesus and to remain faithful in the face of persecution. The white horse represents just this. In fact, whenever you come across the colour white or a crown in the book, you know that this is something or someone on God's side. (Careful though: in one place God's enemies wear false crowns, but the text makes this clear.) The first effect of the exaltation of Messiah Jesus is that the gospel goes out to triumph.

Now the idea of heavenly horses is one we know about from the prophet Zechariah. Those horses reported on what was going on in the world. Sometimes the light of the gospel reveals the true nature of things, and sometimes it can actually provoke violence among those who will not turn to God. And so, the second rider, sent out by the living creature like an ox, carried a sword and took peace from the earth.

Then the third rider was sent out by the creature with a human face, and as so often happens, famine followed in the wake of warfare. The famine was severe but limited. The vine and the olive trees have deep roots and so were unaffected.

The last living creature, the one like an eagle, called, and out went another horse and his rider. This was the pestilence, which follows war and famine as night follows day. Together the three riders, in the light of the gospel represented by the first rider, brought judgement on a quarter of the earth.

6 The martyrs and the end

Revelation 6:9–17

I was still watching all of this from my vantage point in heaven. When the fifth seal was opened, I saw the souls of the martyred under the heavenly altar. They belong there, in the place of sacrifice, because they have followed their Master to the point of death. The martyrs pray for vindication. They long for the day when God will act to show they are in the right, and so make plain his own faithfulness, but they were told that it was not yet time for that. There was still some leeway for their persecutors to change their ways and seek forgiveness, even though this might mean the deaths of more martyrs.

Then the sixth seal was opened, and the end came. Some of the images are drawn from ideas about the destruction of the Jerusalem temple and the tearing of its veil on which the night sky, that is, the visible heavens, was represented. You all know that in the Messiah's own teaching his death is related to the destruction of the temple, which is in turn a sign of the renewal of all things. The vision therefore refers back to the death of Messiah Jesus and then envisages its consequences for those who do not respond to him in repentance and faith. The sky vanished, just as the temple veil was torn, and the people on earth could see directly into the heavenly temple, which meant they were faced with the truth of who they were and what they had done. Every category of humanity tried to run from this revelation, this moment of truth, but found no hiding place. This is the wrath of the Lamb.

Guidelines

- The studies began with seven keys to the interpretation of Revelation. Are there others that ought to have been included? Have any of them been helpful to you in reflecting again on the Bible's final book? What do *you* think John might have said to those who first took the book to the seven churches?
- When you consider the things in the news this week, does your understanding of Revelation help you to see the spiritual realities that lie behind the things being reported? Sometimes it's reassuring to know that however things may appear, Revelation assures us that God is in overall charge of history.
- Some have argued that Revelation shows the way the kingdom petition of the Lord's Prayer will be answered. It shows us how God's kingdom shall come to earth and how his will shall be done here as it already is in the heavenly realm. As you pray the Lord's Prayer, hold the visions of Revelation in your mind and ask God to train your heart and your desires so that they long, above all other things, for his kingdom to come.

28 June–4 July

1 Two pictures of the people of God

Revelation 7

The last vision asked who could stand on the day of wrath, and this vision offers an answer. I saw that judgement was being withheld until the people of God had been identified. The idea of this being done through a seal is borrowed from Ezekiel. The ones marked with a seal are the people of God and are thus the ones who will stand, that is, who will survive the judgement.

Next I heard the number of those who had been marked as God's people. By this point I had grasped that when I heard about things, they would be revealed to me in terms of the fulfilment of the ancient promises as I had once understood them. I was hearing about the great messianic army drawn from all the tribes of Israel. This was the group that would follow the Messiah into battle, defeat the pagans and install their leader in Jerusalem as king of all the kings of the world.

As you all know, the number twelve carries deep significance. It is the number of the tribes and the number of the Messiah's apostles. It is therefore the number of the people of God. 1,000 indicates fullness, and when these are put together and squared to get the figure 144,000, this represents the complete people of God. But remember, this is something I *heard*. The fulfilment of the promise will be revealed in what I *saw*. Even the number 144,000 is trumped by a number that cannot be calculated.

Then I looked and I saw how this ancient promise was being fulfilled. There were people who had been drawn from every nation, and they were gathered in praise around the throne in the heavenly temple. But who were they? It was revealed that these were the ones who had stayed faithful to Messiah Jesus in the face of persecution and even death. This was the fulfilment of God's promises, and it had not been accomplished through warfare but through faithfulness to the way of Messiah Jesus in the face of violence. The multitude was made up of people who had died, and yet, paradoxically, these were the ones who had been able to stand on the day of wrath. Their robes had been washed white in the blood of the Lamb, which means that their sinful deeds had been atoned for and so they need not face judgement, but, having remained true in the face of persecution, they were now part of the people of God.

2 The end gathers pace

Revelation 8

As you read, you will notice that the different visions and sequences of the book do not stand alone but are interweaved into the ones around them. This tells you something important. The visions are not of things that happen in isolation but are integrated into one another. The first and largest part is able to hold all the other parts. In one sense, everything is finished at the end of the vision of the Lamb's exaltation, for the end is described there. In another sense, it is finished at the opening of the sixth seal, when the end is described from a different perspective. Then it finishes again at the sounding of the seventh trumpet, when the world's kingdoms are handed over to God and to his Messiah. The point is that each succeeding vision offers a further account of things that happen within the earlier ones.

When the seventh seal was opened, there was silence in heaven, and then the next sequence was introduced – the angels with trumpets. Only then was the purpose of the silence revealed, which was that it enabled the prayers of the saints to be heard. The covenant signs were then reiterated, indicating that God was keeping his ancient promises. This is an assurance that God hears and acts upon the prayers of his people.

The judgements indicated in the course of the openings of the seals affected a quarter of the earth. Now things are gathering pace and the next judgements impact a third of it. Judgement falls in turn upon the earth, the sea waters, the fresh waters and the visible heavens. The details in the visions indicate that creation itself is coming apart at the seams. Human sin is causing order to unravel, and chaos is emerging again. Perhaps a day will come when humans will persist in behaving in ways that they know are damaging the earth, the seas and the rivers, even when they can see the harm they are doing. All the evidence will be staring them in the face, and yet they will be unable to repent and live differently.

Then an eagle announced three woes that were yet to befall the people of the earth. These are related to the sounding of the last three trumpets. It might seem odd that a bird should proclaim these things, but remember that one of the four creatures that make up God's throne is like an eagle in flight.

3 A plague of locusts

Revelation 9:1–12

The bottomless pit is the Abyss, the place within creation which is the lair of evil and its agents. Later we will see the Monster appear from there. In these visions, this place is related to the sea and to the far side of the river Euphrates, in that evil can emerge from any of them. When God allows evil into creation, it is always limited and subject to his control. In this vision, the opening of the Abyss releases evil into the world as an act of judgement.

The vision combines three of our greatest fears: first the fear of a swarm of locusts that could consume our entire harvest and leave us suffering from famine; next the fear of animals whose sting is fatal; and finally the fear of enemy cavalry, the most dangerous of our foes. These creatures can harm only those who are not a part of the people of God and so are part of God's judgement upon them. These creatures from the pit appear to have crowns but do not.

The time of their activity is limited to five months. While this period relates to the life cycle of the locust, the important point to remember is that it is equivalent to 150 days, which is the time the floodwaters were over the earth in the story in Genesis. That act of judgement came when waters were released from the fountains of the great deep – or the Abyss, as is made clear in the Greek translations of the Hebrew scriptures, with which most of you are familiar. The agents of both acts of judgement emerge from the same place – waters that lead to death in one case and creatures who make their victims long for death in the other case.

These dreadful, monstrous creatures have a king who embodies the character and purpose of the Abyss. He has both a Hebrew name and a Greek one. In Hebrew the name (Abaddon) means destruction and he is a known associate of Belial, one of the names of the archenemy. His Greek name (Apollyon) means destroyer and recalls the name of the pagan 'god' Apollo, whom Nero, that great persecutor of God's people in Rome, took as his patron.

4 The monstrous cavalry

Revelation 9:13–21

I continued to watch all of this from my vantage point in the heavenly temple. I knew that this is where those who were prophets before me had stood to receive their call and be sent out. The sixth trumpet sounded, and things worsened for those who were not a part of the people of God. They had longed for death when attacked by the scorpions, and now it would come for a third of them.

As we have seen, evil can come from the Abyss, but this time it comes from the other side of the Euphrates. Angelic beings who were destined to kill humans were set free. I heard the number of cavalry and saw a vision of the monstrous horses and the way that they brought death.

It was then that I saw more clearly the purpose of all this death and destruction that God was allowing to happen. He had tried everything else. Humans were engaged in undoing the very fabric of creation. There had to be some warning that they would heed. First a quarter of the earth was affected and now a third of humanity. Yet they still would not change their ways. They still make gods of things that are opposed to their own well-being. They persist in giving the highest value to things of their own making. Their chief desire is always something other than the God who made them, who loves them and who longs for them to turn to him so that he can embrace them. But humans choose instead to honour lifeless things that cannot give life. They organise their lives around violence, deception, sex and money, stop at nothing to acquire them and pretend that they are the source of value and meaning. They give them names like security, politics, self-actualisation and the market; and then they honour these things as though they really existed rather than being humanity's own invention and projections of their own desires. They were caught in a cycle of their own making and could not or would not escape whatever God might do. They would surely reap the whirlwind.

5 The call renewed

Revelation 10

I was aware that the seventh trumpet was yet to sound and that the second woe was not yet over, yet at this point something else caught my attention.

It was an enormous angel going down from heaven. The angel was vast. He had one foot on the sea and the other on the land. He wore a cloud around him, and his head reached up to a rainbow in the sky. He reached from earth to heaven. I call him mighty, and like the other mighty angel I had encountered earlier, this one was concerned with a scroll, this time a small one. As Jesus received a scroll from God, I received one from the angel. It is possible that the scrolls were the same ones and that this has been passed to the angel to pass on to me. If so, this makes this scroll the apocalypse given by God to Jesus and then to me via an angel as described at the beginning of the book.

His shout was like the roar of a lion, and I was reminded that one of the creatures who makes up the throne of God is like a lion. He sounded seven thunders and I thought, I'm starting to see the pattern now. We've had six seals then six trumpets, and the next series must be the thunders. They are announced before the seventh trumpet sounds. I recalled the judgements so far – first a quarter and then a third – so these thunders will surely affect half of the earth. I got ready to write it all down but was told not to do so. There could be no further delay; things had to proceed.

Instead of writing, I took the scroll that the angel passed up to me. Remember, I was standing in the heavenly temple and he reached from earth to the skies. The scroll was open, and I thought I would be told to read it. Instead, like Ezekiel, I was told to eat it. I understood that the prophet does not simply speak words from God but that those words are a part of him and affect her personally. The impact would not just be for others but for me. If you, my brothers and sisters are to speak the prophetic word, it should first form you and shape you.

Then the call came to speak about things that are beyond my capacity and experience.

6 The witnesses

I was given a measuring stick, and I knew that this must be a sign of judgement on the temple that I had to go and measure. Its inner courts, including the Holy of Holies, were under judgement, and the outer court would belong to the pagans. We have seen that the number seven is really significant, and so a seven-year period is filled with symbolic meaning. Lots of things in the visions happen for exactly half of that period, which can be expressed as 42 months, 1,260 days or a time (one year), times (two years) and half a time (half a year), making three and a half years.

In the Hebrew scriptures you need two witnesses to bring a charge, and so the people of God who witness through this period are described in language drawn from Zechariah as two witnesses. They have the characteristics of a number of characters from the scriptures, including Moses – who turned the Nile to blood – and Elijah – who called down fire and whose prayers stopped rainfall. They are killed by the Monster that emerges from the Abyss and they lie dead in the city that is opposed to the purposes of God. This has many names in scripture, including Sodom, Egypt and, as we shall see, Babylon. Surprisingly, perhaps, it also includes the earthly Jerusalem, where the authorities turned on Messiah Jesus and executed him.

The witness of the people of God to truth had been a provocation to the peoples of the world, and so they celebrated their demise and found unity in their destruction. However, God's people were taken into heaven. Judgement came in the form of an earthquake that affected a tenth of the city and killed

7,000, but for once it achieved its goal and those who remained glorified God.

This was the end of the second woe, and so the seventh trumpet was sounded. At this point, the end was announced – again – and the elders in heaven praised God. It is interesting to note the reference to God destroying those who destroy the earth. This seems to be an indication that human sin will reach the point where it is adversely affecting creation.

At this point, the earth sees the ark of the covenant within the heavenly temple, and lots of covenant signs remind us that this whole process is about God fulfilling his ancient promises.

Guidelines

- One of the great issues of our day concerns climate change and its effects on the environment. Many of the judgements in Revelation refer to dramatic changes to earthly ecologies, and the destroyers of the earth are among those destroyed by God. Yet humans do not change their ways. Can you think of ways in which Revelation might be used to encourage people to address the behaviours that are causing climate change?
- Some interpret the judgements of Revelation as non-literal descriptions of the impact of human sin when God leaves us to our own devices. Is this a helpful way of viewing things or does God's involvement have to be more direct?
- You might want to read through Mark 13 – or its parallels in Matthew or Luke – which is sometimes called the Synoptic Apocalypse. Can you see any points of parallel or of contrast with Revelation 1—11?

FURTHER READING

R. Bauckham, *The Theology of the Book of Revelation* (CUP, 1993).

R. Bauckham, *The Climax of Prophecy: Studies on the book of Revelation* (Continuum, 1993).

G.K. Beale, *The Book of Revelation* (Eerdmans, 1999).

G.B. Caird, *The Revelation of St John the Divine* (A&C Black, 1966).

E. Corsini, *The Apocalypse: The perennial revelation of Jesus Christ* (Wipf and Stock, 2019).

I. Paul, *How to Read the Book of Revelation* (Grove, 2003).

S. Woodman, *The Book of Revelation* (SCM Press, 2008).

Isaiah 56—66

C.L. Crouch

Isaiah 56—66 is the third major section of the book of Isaiah, which preserves traditions associated with Isaiah ben Amoz together with their interpretation and expansion by later generations. Isaiah 56—66 (also Third Isaiah or Trito-Isaiah) represents the final stage of this process. Its oracles are anonymous; the author (or authors) presents the material as an extension of the Isaianic traditions, but does not claim Isaianic authorship. Contextual clues suggest that these oracles were written down in the late sixth or early fifth centuries BC.

During the final years in Babylonia, another prophet inspired by the traditions of Isaiah ben Amoz had promised that Yahweh was about to return the people to their ancestral homeland and that Jerusalem would be gloriously restored (Isaiah 40—55). It nevertheless surely came as a surprise when a Persian army led by Cyrus II defeated the mighty Babylonian empire, then decreed that the peoples whom the Babylonians had displaced could return to their native lands. Although some stayed in Mesopotamia, others ventured west. In many cases, these migrants were seeing their parents' and grandparents' homeland for the first time.

Expectations were high – bounteous flora and fauna, numerous offspring and Jerusalem itself rebuilt in precious jewels (Isaiah 55). Reality was a disappointment. Yehud was a backwater province of the Persian empire, frequently engaged in petty disputes with its northern neighbours in Samaria. Jerusalem was in ruins. Isaiah 56—66 asks why Isaiah 40—55's promises of a glorious restoration had not been realised. The response draws on the breadth and depth of the Isaianic tradition, identifying failures of justice and righteousness as well as violations of Yahweh's holiness as key impediments to the realisation of Yahweh's kingdom on earth. This anonymous poetry offers a powerful vision of God's radical inclusivity, as it urges us to invite the homeless, the disabled, the poor and the migrant into our communities today.

Unless otherwise stated, Bible quotations and section headings are taken from the CEB.

1 Keepers of God's sabbath

Isaiah 56:1–8

Third Isaiah begins with a pair of imperatives that sum up the heart of its message: 'Act justly and do what is righteous' (v. 1). The point of the declaration as an opening salvo is clear: the people's failure to keep these two simple commands is key to understanding their present situation. These are not new commandments, of which the people might claim to have been unaware: exhortations to do justice and enact righteousness occur throughout the Isaianic traditions. The song of the vineyard identifies bloodshed in place of justice and cries of oppression in lieu of righteousness as the cause of the people's destruction (Isaiah 5; compare 10:2; 28:17).

In Isaiah 40—55, the foremost responsibility of Yahweh's servant is to 'bring forth justice', not only in Israel but also among the nations (Isaiah 42:1, 3–4; compare 51:1, 4). Isaiah 56—66 takes up these traditions, affirming their relevance to the current generation. If the people want to understand what has gone wrong, here is their first clue.

Yet (one might protest), 'justice' and 'righteousness' are very general virtues. What do they mean in concrete terms? The following verses offer specific examples: to 'act justly' and to 'do what is righteous' means to welcome the immigrant and the disabled into the community as full and equal members. The oracle's use of quotations signals that this was a shocking declaration to its first hearers. Ezekiel 44:6–9 identifies the admission of foreigners into the temple as one of the causes of Judah's destruction and the people's deportation. Deuteronomy 23:2 prohibits any male whose genitalia have been damaged from entering Yahweh's sanctuary. But Isaiah 56 declares, that 'the eunuchs who keep my sabbaths, choose what I desire, and remain loyal to my covenant' (v. 4) and 'the immigrants who have joined me, serving me and loving my name' (v. 6) will be accepted by Yahweh when they approach the most sacred precincts of Yahweh's temple in Jerusalem (v. 7).

Yahweh's expansive inclusivity is captured by the repetition of *qbṣ*, 'to gather' (v. 8). Notably, Yahweh's present activities are grounded in Yahweh's past actions on Israel's behalf (compare Isaiah 43:1–2; 48:21; 51:2, etc.). This passage is invoked by the modern state of Israel's Yad VaShem memorial: it is 'a monument and a name' (v. 5) for those who died in the Holocaust.

2 Neglectful leaders

Part of the problem is that the people are convinced that they have all the time in the world to amend their ways. Why trouble oneself with change when 'tomorrow will be like today' (56:12)? The vivid imagery of this oracle unpacks the warning implied by the opening summons to do what is righteous and just (56:1). Yahweh 'is coming soon' to judge the people for their behaviour – but will find the people lazing about drinking (56:12)!

The Bible generally assumes that its audience consumes alcohol – almost a necessity in an era before water sanitation – and even includes it among God's good provisions for humanity (Psalm 104:15; Isaiah 25:6; 55:1). Like many good gifts, however, wine and beer can be problematic when consumed to excess (Proverbs 23:29–35; Ephesians 5:18). The prophets often use drunkenness to describe the selfish behaviour of a community's leadership – those who prioritise their own individual enjoyment rather than the well-being of those for whom they are responsible (Isaiah 5:11–13; 24:7–11; 28:1, 7; Jeremiah 25:15; Joel 1:5; Amos 2:8; 6:6; Habakkuk 2:5).

The confluence of images in this passage suggests that Israel's leaders are acting like besotted idiots – like a person so drunk that his mental faculties resemble those of domestic animals (56:9–10). They are like a watchdog caught sleeping on the job after a greedy meal (v. 11). Yet Yahweh's accusation concerns more than mere neglect; these dogs have 'monstrous appetites' (v. 11). These shepherds actively work to the detriment of the flock with which they have been entrusted (compare Ezekiel 34). Moreover, their vision is so obscured that they fail to notice their shortcomings – even when they result in death (57:1). The passage concludes on a brief note of reassurance for the victims; though they may have been denied peace in life, they will find it in death (57:2).

3 Accusations against idolaters

The description of the idolaters as 'offspring of adultery and prostitution' is unlikely to be literal (v. 3). Several of the prophets make extensive use of a metaphorical frame in which the people's loyalty to Yahweh is likened to a woman's loyalty to her husband; its disloyalty is akin to adultery (Hosea 1—3; Jeremiah 3; Ezekiel 16; 23). (The Bible tends to elide adultery and prostitution, as two forms of unrestrained female sexuality.) The metaphor poses certain ethical difficulties (on which see C.L. Crouch, 'Hosea', *Guidelines* 35:2 [2019], pp. 46–68), but it explains why the worship of gods other than Yahweh is depicted as a violation of sexual exclusivity (not, we should emphasise, because ancient sanctuaries were full of 'sacred prostitutes', for which the evidence is vanishingly small).

Although less explicit than many of its predecessors – Ezekiel 16 and 23 verge on the pornographic – these verses continue this rhetorical tradition when they depict the people's religious behaviour as though it were elaborate seduction scene. (From verse 7 onward, 'you' is feminine singular.)

Here, as elsewhere, these accusations carry undertones of political disloyalty, as well as religious apostasy. When the people are described as 'making room in your bed', the issue is not only that they are welcoming other gods but that they are cosying up to the people who worship those gods (v. 8). When it describes them as 'making deals' and 'sending messengers far away', it depicts them as seeking out and relying on political alliances rather, than Yahweh (vv. 8–9). The perception of such machinations as antithetical to Yahwistic worship had been a prominent theme of the messages of Isaiah ben Amoz, who viewed Judah's kings' reliance on foreign powers as an indication that they lacked confidence in Yahweh's power and protection (Isaiah 7—8).

When verse 9 speaks of sending messengers as far as the underworld, it invokes Isaiah ben Amoz's condemnation of alliances with Egypt, which are depicted as a covenant with Death (playing on the similarity of the Hebrew for death, *môt*, and the name of the Egyptian goddess Mut). The world of Isaiah 57 was a similarly international one; the people had spent decades in a foreign country, surrounded by foreign gods. (The word 'abandoned' in verse 8 uses *glh*, the same word for 'exile'.) Verse 11 alludes, perhaps, to the people's estrangement from Yahweh in Babylonia, suggesting that they abandoned Yahweh because they thought Yahweh had abandoned them.

4 Peace for the remorseful

The latter half of the chapter contains further echoes of earlier Isaianic material. Several terms in the summons to 'build a road! Remove barriers from my people's road!' (v. 14) repeat those in the more famous 'Clear [Yahweh's] way in the desert! Make a level highway in the wilderness for our God' (Isaiah 40:3). Here the 'way' (*derek*) is explicitly for 'my people'; in Isaiah 40, comfort is promised to 'my people', but the purpose of the way in the wilderness is to draw attention to Yahweh's return to Zion, rather than the people's. The echo here suggests that, though Yahweh has returned to Zion, the people have yet to do so, at least metaphorically – they continue 'wandering wherever they wanted' (v. 17). Further attention from Yahweh will be required; yet again, Yahweh's willingness to shower gracious gifts upon the people has not prompted the appropriate thanksgiving but rather greed and misattribution of the source of their abundance (v. 17).

The text acknowledges that Yahweh 'withdrew' from the people in anger – so frustrated with their behaviour that presence among them was temporarily impossible (compare Ezekiel 11). The utter abandonment occasioned by this divine retreat is expressed with utmost anguish in the book of Lamentations, in which Yahweh makes no response to the cries of Jerusalem and its inhabitants. This section acts as a reminder that, as Yahweh relented before – 'Comfort, comfort my people' (Isaiah 40:1) – so Yahweh will relent again. This is cast as an act of absolute divine sovereignty. Yahweh is 'the one who is high and lifted up, who lives forever, whose name is holy' (v. 15) – phraseology familiar from Isaiah ben Amoz's vision of Yahweh enthroned in the temple (6:1; compare 33:10; 49:22; 52:13; and contrast 2:12–14; 37:23 concerning those who challenge this power).

This holiness is invoked in a striking assertion: not only does it mean that Yahweh 'lives on high in holiness' – that is, as the supreme and sovereign deity over all that one might expect – but that Yahweh dwells also 'with the crushed and the lowly'. The Hebrew root used for 'crushed' (*dk'*) is the same used to describe the servant in 53:5. Both passages assert Yahweh's solidarity with the marginalised: the holy and sovereign God of the universe deigns to dwell alongside the least powerful among us, seeking justice on their behalf.

5 Fasting from injustice

Isaiah 58 takes aim at the people's ostentatious displays of piety. The 'house of Jacob' (v. 1) is an alternative name for the 'house of Israel' (compare Genesis 32; 35), especially common in the book of Isaiah. This reflects the special resonance of the Jacob story with the experience of the book's later audiences, as the ancestor who spends most of his adult life away from home. The book in its final form, together with much of its contents, was composed for migrants – the involuntarily displaced migrants to Babylonia and the return migrants to the homeland. The oracles in Isaiah 40—55 suggest that the former had made a special connection with Jacob; they are repeatedly called 'Jacob', as they are summoned to return home (40:27; 41:8, etc.; compare 41:21; 49:26, in which Yahweh is called 'Jacob's king' and the 'mighty one of Jacob').

Isaiah 58's description of its audience as the 'house of Jacob' identifies them as those deportees' descendants ('house' is a common way of describing a person's family). But these heirs of Yahweh's promises to Jacob are demanding all the benefits of this relationship with Yahweh while being unwilling to act in a way appropriate to that relationship (v. 2). Instead of seeking justice for those abused by the powerful, Yahweh's people are putting on a show of piety and pursuing violence among themselves (vv. 3–4).

Then, as now, refraining from food and other activities was meant to prompt a person to meditate on Yahweh – every twinge of the stomach a reminder that the source of the grain, the wine and the oil is Yahweh alone. Such time should prompt greater awareness of Yahweh's nature and the desire to act in ways that reflect it – not serve as a demonstration of piety for the neighbours (v. 5). The people are going through the motions, but missing the point (vv. 3, 13).

Yahweh is a God who cares for the poor, the homeless, the mistreated, the naked; Yahweh's people must do so as well (vv. 6–7, 9). When they align themselves rightly with Yahweh, then Yahweh will align Godself with them – the promises of restoration made to their ancestors in exile will also be theirs (vv. 10, 14; compare 42:6, 16; 49:6; 51:4).

6 Alienation from God

The people claim that Yahweh is ignoring them (58:3), but that is not the problem: Yahweh can hear perfectly well and is more than powerful enough to intervene (v. 1). The problem is that the people's behaviour is inappropriate to proximity to the divine (v. 2). Indeed, the people are not only failing to act righteously (Isaiah 58), but they are also actively pursuing wickedness. Especially prominent in this passage are sins associated with speech and verbal testimony: 'Your lips speak lies; your tongues mutter malice… no one pleads truthfully… speaking deceit' (vv. 3–4).

The Bible's strenuous opposition to false witness is attested prominently in the legal material (Exodus 20:16; 23:7; Leviticus 6:3; 19:12; Deuteronomy 5:20; 19:18), but it appears also in the psalms and the prophets as an especially offensive crime (Isaiah 9:15; 32:7; 57:4; Jeremiah 5:2, 31; etc.). Accustomed as we are to 'white lies' and other half-truths, the penalties invoked for these offences strike us as extreme: the psalmist, in one memorable example, pleads with Yahweh to 'break the teeth in their mouths' (Psalm 58:6).

The alarm raised by such behaviour is more comprehensible in a context with no criminal forensics; in a court of law, the reliability of a person's word was everything. The accusation laid at the people's door in this passage is more than a grumble about fibs: these lies are undermining the community's entire justice system. False accusations and criminal cover-ups all but guarantee miscarriages of justice; the innocent will receive the punishment while the real perpetrators walk free. In a legal system reliant on corporal and capital punishments (there are no prisons until much later), these lies are harbingers of death – hence the vivid language of deadly spiders lying in wait for the unsuspecting and vipers about to strike (v. 5).

The climactic final verses imply that these offences are not even for personal gain, merely the work of malevolent troublemakers who occupy themselves with evil (vv. 6–8).

Guidelines

The book of Isaiah's emphasis on justice and righteousness among the people – or, more often, their failure to achieve it – is linked to its conception of Yahweh, the people's God. As Isaiah ben Amoz put it, '[Yahweh of hosts] will be exalted in justice, and the holy God will show himself holy in righteousness' (5:16, compare 30:18; 33:5; 40:14).

In Third Isaiah, the connection between Yahweh's character and the moral expectations of the people is affirmed immediately, in the opening verse: 'Do what is righteous, because my salvation is coming soon, and my righteousness will be revealed' (56:1). Justice and righteousness are essential aspects of Yahweh's character. Because Israel is Yahweh's special people, they must pursue justice and righteousness also. They must also be holy, so that they may approach their superlatively holy deity (compare Leviticus 11:44–45: 'Be holy, because I am holy'). Such holiness is achieved through the pursuit of justice and righteousness.

The repeated exhortations to this effect reflect the importance of the imitation of God (*imitatio Dei*) as a core principle of Isaiah's theological ethics. Although the people are not gods – far from it! – they demonstrate their commitment to Yahweh by demonstrating their commitment to the values Yahweh holds most significant.

Indeed, these values provide the framework for Yahweh's own activities: Yahweh acts to ensure that justice is done and righteousness is upheld. From the perspective of the oppressed, this is good news; they will be vindicated. From the perspective of the oppressor, it should be terrifying; Yahweh, God-self, will intervene in judgement. As with our predecessors, we are too often prone to put off our pursuit of justice until tomorrow; the book of Isaiah warns us that to do so is to invoke the wrath of a deity whose very being is one committed to justice. If we do not 'act justly and do what is righteous' – welcome the foreigner and the disabled into our communities, housing the homeless, clothing the naked, feeding the hungry – then we fail to follow the God for whom these matter more than all the churchgoing, prayers and tithes we can muster.

1 Injustice obscures vision

Isaiah 59:9–15a

Isaiah 59:9 shifts into a first-person voice, encouraging the people to acknowledge their participation in and corporate responsibility for the shortcomings declared in the preceding verses – subversions of justice by word and by deed (59:3–8). The passage confesses that it is because we work actively against justice and eschew righteous behaviour that 'justice is far' and 'righteousness beyond our reach' (v. 9). Our invocations of Yahweh's power to intervene for justice are subverted by our own injustices; we expect Yahweh to act on our behalf, without wanting to admit that Yahweh's justice will invoke judgement on ourselves as well.

The natural imagery echoes the warnings of Amos about the 'day of Yahweh' that the people foolishly desire: 'Why do you want the day of [Yahweh]? It is darkness, not light; as if someone fled from a lion, and was met by a bear; or sought refuge in a house, rested a hand against the wall, and was bitten by a snake' (Amos 5:18–20). The day that we thought would bring Yahweh's action in our favour and judgement on our enemies has turned out to be a day of judgement on us. We confess that this is a consequence of our numerous sins, described in the language of blindness familiar from elsewhere in Isaiah (29:9, 18; 35:5; 42:7, 16, 18–19; 43:8; also and especially the instructions to Isaiah ben Amoz in 6:10).

Whereas Isaiah 56:10 emphasised the blindness of the leaders, verse 10 widens the net to include the whole community – all have fallen short. These verses constitute a declaration of guilt – a public acknowledgement of the problem and a necessary prelude to change. One of the centremost elements of the traditional liturgy is a confession of this kind, in which we admit that we frequently fail to act in a way consonant with God's will and ask for Yahweh's help in changing our behaviour. In the secular sphere, a similar principle lies at the heart of addiction recovery organisations' methods: all the well-meaning family and friends in the world can do only limited good if a person is unwilling to admit that they have a problem.

2 God will intervene

After the catastrophe of the exile, the prophets concluded that Israel's relationship with Yahweh could no longer depend on Israel's ability to keep all of Yahweh's commandments reliably. The only way forward was an 'everlasting' or 'eternal' covenant' (55:3; 61:8; Jeremiah 32:40; Ezekiel 16:60; 37:26; compare Jeremiah 31:31–34; 33:20–22). This passage affirms that principle, culminating in the declaration that Yahweh's spirit will not depart from the mouths of the people or of their descendants (v. 21). The Hebrew word for 'spirit' in verse 21 is *ruah*; it is the same word used in verse 19 for 'the Lord's wind'. Verse 21's promise of a persistent covenant with Yahweh is thus directly connected to the depiction of Yahweh's actions in the preceding verses, in which Yahweh acts to ensure the justice the people are failing to achieve.

Yahweh's promise of an eternal covenant is a double-edged sword. Yahweh will ultimately ensure that justice is done, even if we fail in our mortal efforts to achieve it. Yet this is no carte blanche – the perpetrators of injustice may be certain of an ultimate divine reckoning. The entire passage brings out the extent to which the divine character traits highlighted elsewhere – justice and righteousness – dominate Yahweh's interventions in the earthly realm, going so far as to describe Yahweh as 'putting on righteousness as armour' in preparation for that divine reckoning (v. 17).

Although the juxtaposition of Yahweh as warrior and Yahweh as righteous judge may seem incongruous to us, in the ancient world both of these functions were closely connected to kingship. A good king was responsible for ensuring the welfare of his people; this was achieved by protecting the realm from those who sought to invade and oppress it and by establishing the necessary mechanisms for justice, then ensuring that they operated fairly. One of the psalmists offers a good summary of this ideal king, as he prays for the one he has: 'Let the king bring justice to people who are poor, let him save the children of those who are needy, but let him crush oppressors!... Let the king rule from sea to sea, from the river to the ends of the earth' (Psalm 72:4, 8). This human ideal is modelled on Yahweh's role as divine king; what human kings aspired to do on behalf of their people, Yahweh actually does.

3 Jerusalem's coming radiance

Isaiah 60 revisits the images of restoration that feature in Isaiah 40—55, reaffirming that Yahweh's promises to the people are still valid. The centre of attention is the city of Jerusalem, which is imagined metaphorically as a mother deprived of her children. Unlike in earlier times, in which powerful nations overshadowed Jerusalem and deported her inhabitants to foreign lands, now the situation will be reversed: no longer will Jerusalem be overshadowed, but rather her glory will shine out with such brightness that all the nations around will see it. The command that Jerusalem must 'Shine!' because her 'light has come' (v. 1) invokes once more the metaphors of sight and blindness that recur throughout the book as indicators of the people's response (or lack thereof) to Yahweh's desire for justice.

The chapter's resonance with the promises of Isaiah 40—55 in particular evoke the description of Yahweh's servant there: Yahweh's chosen servant is the one who is 'called in righteousness' as 'a light to the nations' and who is commissioned to bring the justice that liberates prisoners and those whose lives are full of darkness (42:1, 6–7, compare 49:6, 9). So, too, in Isaiah 60 the light that comes from Yahweh is one that overcomes darkness with liberation as its aim.

Jerusalem's children, who have been held captive among the nations for a generation or more, will be freed to come home (v. 4). But this liberating power will not be limited to Yahweh's special people; Jerusalem's light will attract the people of other nations as well (vv. 4, 10–11). The exertion of dominance that once characterised these nations' attitudes will no longer hold; they will repent of their oppression and grant Jerusalem the honour it is due. This honour is not a response to Jerusalem's own merit; rather, it arises from the presence of Yahweh in the temple on Mount Zion. The gifts and tribute brought to the city by the nations are destined for the temple, where they pale in comparison to the glory of the Holy One of Israel (vv. 5–7, 9).

4 Joyful proclamations

Isaiah 61 continues with this vision of a future in which Jerusalem (Zion), and its orientation towards Yahweh, is the source of international justice. Good news for the poor and liberation for prisoners are reaffirmed as litmus tests of society's commitment to justice. They continue as such today. Our overflowing prisons full of poor people – especially those of colour – and an economic system that considers human beings useful only insofar as they contribute to gross domestic product – and discards them on the streets when they cannot – stand convicted by Isaiah's vision of God's kingdom.

The promise of a double portion (v. 7) recalls the announcement in 40:2 that Jerusalem's 'penalty has been paid… she has received from the Lord's hand double for all her sins'. Both announcements probably draw on legal principles governing the restoration of community equilibrium after a violation (as in Exodus 22:1, 7, 9) and are a way of expressing the perfect resolution of Jerusalem's previous suffering. Yahweh's covenant with Israel is now explicitly an 'eternal' or 'enduring' one (v. 8). The Hebrew ('ôlam) connotes duration at the limits of human ability to conceive: thus is Yahweh's commitment to the people. This is not permission for the people to act in any way they like, but rather an affirmation of Yahweh's ongoing determination to see justice and righteousness fulfilled among them.

The opening lines speak of Zion's mourners and promise that they will once more be filled with joy and praise. The devastation of the city had not only left its people scattered and bereft – the book of Lamentations speaks powerfully of the despair felt by survivors – but it had also called Yahweh's very character into question. Yahweh's decision to bring Nebuchadnezzar against Jerusalem had been an act determined by a commitment to justice, insofar as the people's sins had gone unpunished for so long that Yahweh appeared either unable or uninterested in just judgement; Yahweh's actions affirmed that evil deeds must have consequences. But the subsequent suffering of the people at the hands of their enemies called Yahweh's justice into question again. Yahweh's extension of comfort to all who lament this suffering thus vindicates Yahweh's character as a God committed to justice (vv. 2–3).

5 Jerusalem redeemed

Isaiah 62

The description of Jerusalem before and after its restoration highlights the reputational element of Yahweh's actions. The city's devastation has led to verbal abuse from the nations, who have declared that the city must have been 'Abandoned' and 'Deserted' by its God (v. 4). This is why it stands deserted of people: they too have abandoned the city. Isaiah 62 rejects this interpretation and affirms Jerusalem's special status in Yahweh's care: henceforth the city will be called the 'City That Is Not Abandoned', the one of whom Yahweh has declared, 'My Delight Is in Her' (vv. 12, 4). The nations will see Jerusalem's revitalisation and recognise that Yahweh's actions had been for the sake of filling Jerusalem with righteousness (v. 1).

One of Jerusalem's new names, 'Married' (v. 4), inverts the tragic outcomes typical of other appearances of the marriage metaphor – those in which Yahweh declared that Israel 'is not my wife, and I am not her husband' (Hosea 2:2) or 'sent unfaithful Israel away with divorce papers' (Jeremiah 3:8). The chapter, like those preceding, restates promises made in Isaiah 40—55. In verse 4, the divorce between Yahweh and the people is denied and forgotten (compare 50:1; 54:4–8); the city will again be full of joyous children (compare 49:19–22; 54:1–3) and akin to a bride (compare 49:18; 54:5–6).

Some of these metaphors worked better in an ancient, patriarchal culture than they do today, insofar as they presuppose circumscribed gender roles and an unequal distribution of power between husband and wife. They continue to function positively where they foreground the extreme care expected of each party in the relationship; in Isaiah 62, Jerusalem is told to lobby Yahweh insistently – 'don't allow God to rest'! (v. 7) – if she is not treated with honour and respect. The metaphor is more problematic when it veers towards depicting Yahweh as a chronically abusive spouse, vacillating between violence and affection.

Taken as positively as possible, Isaiah 62 envisions the violent history between Yahweh and Jerusalem as a tragic interlude, never to be repeated (v. 8; Hebrew *šb'* signifies a solemn oath, stronger than 'promised' suggests). With the affirmation of the covenant between them as eternal, Yahweh surrenders violence as a means of communication and swears to delight in Jerusalem perpetually, as a young man delights in his bride (v. 5).

6 Vengeance against the nations

These verses are shocking: they depict a first-person speaker – presumably Yahweh – wreaking terrible violence upon foreigners, namely, the people of Edom. This is one of several oracles against Edom in prophetic texts from the sixth century BC or later, after Jerusalem's defeat by Nebuchadnezzar (Isaiah 34; Jeremiah 49:7–22; Ezekiel 35; Obadiah). The unusual fury they vent in Edom's direction relates to the Edomites' involvement in the downfall of Jerusalem.

Although the Edomites' exact crime is nowhere fully spelled out, Ezekiel justifies Yahweh's judgement by saying, 'You nursed an ancient grudge, you handed the Israelites over to the sword in the time of their distress, during their final punishment… You said, "These two nations and these two territories are mine. We will take possession of them even if [Yahweh] is there"' (Ezekiel 35:5, 10). The gist of the offence, then, appears to have been an Edomite eagerness to take advantage of Judah's distress for its own gain, rather than come to its aid.

The gravity of the crime was heightened by a perceived family relationship between the Edomites and the Israelites, traditionally articulated in terms of their respective descents from the brothers Esau and Jacob (Genesis 25). The weight given to fraternal loyalty in the ancient world was such that the relationship between the parties to a treaty could be described as 'brothers', with the expectation that the contracting parties treat each other as such (compare Amos 1:11–12, which may stem from this same period). Edom and Judah may have had a formal alliance in the final years of Judah's existence (Jeremiah 27:3), but even without one the Edomites held the status of family in the minds of Jerusalem's inhabitants.

The betrayal of these fraternal loyalties provoked acute anger. Elsewhere in Isaiah, they are a people 'doomed for destruction' as a result (34:5; this chapter is usually understood to be contemporary with Isaiah 40—55 or Isaiah 56—66). In Isaiah 63, this oracle of Edom's destruction is deliberately located with the promises of Jerusalem's restoration: those who helped to destroy it in 586 BC will now themselves be destroyed.

The text is clear, however, that this vengeance upon the Edomites is Yahweh's doing alone: there was no helper or supporter there to assist (v. 5). Yahweh alone is the ultimate – and ultimately sole – guarantor of justice. While the passage affirms Yahweh's commitment to justice, it warns that mortals with limited vision must not arrogate to themselves this power of life and death; that power lies with Yahweh alone.

Guidelines

A nationalist reading of these chapters would view Jerusalem's future in triumphalist terms, identifying the capitals of our own nations with Jerusalem and longing for the subordination of other nations, communities and individuals to our own private domination. The 'foreigners will rebuild your walls, and their kings will serve you', as 60:10 has it. But this would be to miss the thrust of the passage, which is suffused with a vision of justice that will not allow for such abuses of power. Again and again, the vision presented is one that recognises and rectifies past injustices – but does so in pursuit of an international equilibrium governed by justice, not simply a new arrangement of the hierarchy. The foreigners who destroyed Jerusalem's walls will atone by rebuilding them.

Those who believed that they ought to be served by others will heed the call to serve others themselves (60:10). Those who had been the least – the poor, the lowly, the weak, with whom Yahweh most identifies (56:3–7; 57:15) – will find their tormenters at their feet seeking forgiveness (60:14). There will be no more violence (60:18). This vision of Jerusalem as a model of international justice identifies Yahweh's sanctuary – and the orientation of not only Jerusalem but of all the nations towards it – as the source of these renewed relations. The one true overlord, the one being with a rightful claim to reign over humanity, is Yahweh Godself.

There are, to be sure, some parts of Isaiah 56–66's articulation of this vision that rightly make us uncomfortable – the scene of Yahweh's blood-stained destruction of Edom foremost among them. Yet, even there, the words with which Yahweh's authority is affirmed warn against the temptation to grant ourselves licence to go rampaging around the nations wreaking vengeance for perceived slights. Even the most egregious offence is not given to us to avenge; to Yahweh alone belongs that right.

Indeed, in the overall scheme of these oracles the image of Yahweh as warrior is almost entirely subsumed by the emphasis on Yahweh's commitment to justice. As the ultimate and absolute divine king, Yahweh's military aspect is subordinate to Yahweh's determination to pursue justice, rather than an end in itself. Would that we agitate in our own communities for such priorities, seeking justice for the poor, the homeless, the foreigner and the disabled, rather than lust after domination.

1 Prayer of yearning

Isaiah 63:7—64:12

This prayer shifts between pleas for Yahweh to intervene on the people's behalf and recollections of Yahweh's previous saving actions. Assertions that Yahweh has the power to save, using Israel's history as evidence, is typical of the rhetorical style of Isaiah 40—55. There, affirmations of Yahweh's creative and historical powers undergird efforts to persuade the Babylonian community that Yahweh will rescue them (40:12–17, 26; 41:2–4; 42:5; 43:1–2, 16–17; 44:24). They are also typical of the psalms, which detail Yahweh's intervention on the Israelites' behalf as they fled oppression in Egypt (Psalm 78:12–28; 105:26–45; 106:8–12). When Isaiah 63:7 announces an intention to praise Yahweh for 'all [Yahweh] did for us, for God's great favour towards the house of Israel', it is situated within a tradition that links praise of Yahweh with expressions of confidence that Yahweh will continue to act on the people's behalf. Isaiah 63 invokes the exodus (vv. 11–13; compare 64:3–4), emphasising its power to recall Yahweh to action (v. 10).

After several verses of historical recitation, the prayer finally pleads with Yahweh directly, asking Yahweh to remember the people again (v. 15). Among the more striking images is a repeated acclamation of Yahweh as Israel's father (63:16; 64:8). Juxtaposed with acclamations of Yahweh's power over creation (63:15; 64:1–3, 8) and of Yahweh's lordship over heaven and earth (63:15), this recalls the creation of humanity, in which the gift of the divine image signifies Yahweh's parental relationship with these new beings (Genesis 1:26–27; compare Genesis 5:1–4).

Yahweh is more reliable than forgetful human fathers, however; the familial responsibility held by the '[kinsman-]redeemer' is prominently mentioned (63:16). On the heels of a reminder of the fraternal betrayal of Edom (63:1–6), the comment implicitly suggests that Yahweh's abandonment of Jerusalem, its people and its sanctuary was a violation of God's family responsibilities – which Yahweh must act swiftly to rectify. The prophet recognises that Yahweh's perceived forgetfulness was a response to the people's persistence in sin (63:10; 64:5–7), but he asks Yahweh to take pity on the children Yahweh created and restore Jerusalem, in order that they may praise Yahweh in the temple again (64:11).

The prayer ends with a lament over Yahweh's continued silence (64:12, compare, at greater length, the book of Lamentations).

2 Judgement for idolaters

Isaiah 65:1–16

Yahweh's response is probably not what those seeking a mighty demonstration of Yahweh's power were hoping for. 'I was here', says Yahweh, 'but you were looking elsewhere' (vv. 1–2). Although past precedent prompts us to expect the familiar complaint about the people chasing after other deities instead of worshipping the one true God, the words placed in the mouths of the offenders suggest that the main accusation is religious arrogance (v. 5). These people may well believe that they are worshipping Yahweh (though the reference to unclean meats in verse 4 suggests that, if so, they are doing so in a way shunned by biblical authors with purity concerns), but their supposedly pious practices have become an end in themselves; this obsessive concern to preserve their holiness makes it idolatrous.

The oracle goes on to declare, however, that these idolaters' sins will not provoke judgement upon the whole people. As in a previous generation, the prophet insists that Yahweh punishes only those whose actions demand it (Ezekiel 18; though note the recognition elsewhere that one may suffer without cause, as Job was understood to do). Those who choose the futile pursuit of false powers in lieu of worship at Yahweh's holy mountain will suffer as a result; Yahweh has warned them against such offences and they have elected to pursue these evil deeds anyway (v. 11). But punishment will not be the whole story: those who respond to Yahweh's call will be spared judgement (compare Ezekiel 34).

This passage's depiction of divisions within the community is a striking one, and is certainly part of Isaiah 56—66's attempts to explain the delay in Jerusalem's restoration. Though Yahweh has extended grace to the entire community, some have failed to respond appropriately, and it is the stubborn refusal of these people to recognise the source of their good fortune that hinders complete restoration.

The depiction of the chosen as 'servants' signals their close relationship with Yahweh; Abraham (Genesis 18:3–4), Jacob (Genesis 32:10) and Moses (Exodus 4:10, etc.) are all so-called. It also signals a transformation of promises made in Isaiah 40—55. There, though an individual can be called Yahweh's servant (42:1), the title encompasses all of Israel (41:8–9, etc.). Isaiah 65 marks a narrowing of the term: though a close relationship with Yahweh is offered to all, only some choose to take the offer up.

3 New creation and new Jerusalem

Isaiah 65:17–25

Isaiah 65 depicts Yahweh as creator in terms familiar from Isaiah 40—55. There, similar invocations establish Yahweh's authoritative power over the whole universe, seeking to persuade the Israelites that Yahweh's intention to exert it on their behalf is plausible (40:12; 42:5). Isaiah 65 assumes this argumentative background and turns to the future – to the new creation Yahweh is making for the people.

The terms in which this new creation is described draw on traditions about penalties for disloyalty to a suzerain. Verse 21 promises that 'they will build houses and live in them; they will plant vineyards and eat their fruit', which directly annuls a pair of curses in Deuteronomy 28:30: 'You might build a house, but you won't get to live in it. You might plant a vineyard, but you won't enjoy it.' These are futility curses, envisioning a state of affairs in which effort is expended in vain. Several more such curses appear in Deuteronomy 28. A similar, though not identical, warning appears in Esarhaddon's Succession Treaty: 'May your sons not take possession of your house, but a strange enemy divide your goods.'

In Deuteronomy 28, curses depict the evil that will befall the Israelites if they fail to keep Yahweh's commandments, laid out in the preceding chapters. They have a similar function as other ancient agreements, warning especially of the consequences for breaking promises of loyalty. Judah's kings swore such oaths of loyalty to various foreign kings, first the Assyrians and then the Babylonians. When Judah's kings betrayed their oaths to the Babylonian king, Jerusalem was destroyed. The disasters inflicted upon it were understood as reprisals in keeping with the curses laid out in the treaty to which they had sworn. These oaths would have been sworn in Yahweh's name; as a result, Jerusalem's destruction was also understood as the result of the kings' (and people's) failure to be loyal to Yahweh (see Ezekiel 17). The devastation was accordingly articulated with reference to the curses in Deuteronomy. The houses the people had built in Jerusalem and the vineyards planted in Judah were of no use in Babylonia (Lamentations 5:2). Curses that spoke of horrifying acts of cannibalism by starving parents (Deuteronomy 28:53, 56–57) had come to pass (Lamentations 2:20; 4:10).

But Isaiah 65 declares that these horrors are in the past. The new creation will be even more wonderful than the last – even the curse that humanity would labour for food will be overturned (v. 23, compare Genesis 3:17–19)!

4 Where God may be found

Isaiah 66:1–6

Isaiah 66 appears initially to be a further paean to Yahweh's creative power, depicting Yahweh as so great and so powerful that no earthly house could possibly contain such majesty. But its purpose is to deny the authority of the temple, by declaring that Yahweh was too great to be contained within it. ('House' is a common term for temple, as in the discussion over whether David is to build one for Yahweh in 2 Samuel 7.)

Yahweh was ordinarily understood to be 'enthroned upon the cherubim' – first in the tabernacle, then in the temple (Exodus 25:18–22; 37:7–8; 1 Kings 7—8) – although the vision of Isaiah ben Amoz suggests that Yahweh was imagined as so large that merely 'the hem of his robe filled the temple' (6:1, NRSV). This perhaps explains why several times the temple is described as Yahweh's 'footstool' (Psalm 99:5; Lamentations 2:1; 1 Chronicles 28:2). Although the temple was probably not thought to contain Yahweh fully, then, Isaiah 66 uses the limitations of its architecture and an expansive creation theology to conclude that it is inadequate as an abode for Yahweh (vv. 1–2). The passage is later invoked by Stephen to defend a similarly expansive notion of divine presence (Acts 7).

In Isaiah 66, it forms the basis of a case against the temple cult, arguing that humility and contrition are more valuable to Yahweh than offerings and animal sacrifices (v. 2). Although declared in more extreme terms (v. 3) than most such complaints, prophetic protestations concerning rote religious ritual were not new. Amos relates Yahweh's hatred of offerings when presented in the absence of justice and righteousness (Amos 5:21–25); in the Isaianic tradition they are described as burdensome to Yahweh (1:10–17). Sacrificial offerings are nevertheless hardly rejected wholesale; Isaiah 43:22–24 complains that the Israelites have brought Yahweh their sins rather than their sacrifices, while Isaiah 56:6–7 uses temple service and sacrifices to indicate the fullness of the foreigners' and eunuchs' inclusion. Verses 3–4 suggest that the problem is a failure to listen for Yahweh's voice and respond to Yahweh's will. Those unable to recognise Yahweh's summons to live according to the new creation will find that their reliance on mindless rituals brings about catastrophe (v. 6).

5 Mother Zion

Isaiah 66:7–17

A vision of Jerusalem in painless childbirth signals the radical departure of Yahweh's new creation from the realities of the old (vv. 7–8). The children are the city's inhabitants; their easy delivery is a sign of its renewed population. Although the exact state of Jerusalem after 586BC is not well understood, it is clear that the Babylonians destroyed the temple (2 Kings 25:9; Jeremiah 52:13; Lamentations 2:1–7) and that the provincial administration was relocated to Mizpah (Jeremiah 40—41). There are some indications that lamentation or other liturgical practices were sustained at the site of the temple while it lay in ruins (Jeremiah 41:5; the book of Lamentations), but the city surrounding it remained small and impoverished well into the Persian period.

The extent to which depopulation was viewed as an affront to the city's proper status may be seen in Lamentations, which takes the image of the empty city as paradigmatic of its desolation: 'She sits alone, the city that was once full of people' (Lamentations 1:1). Even after some of the descendants of the people deported from the city in 597BC and 586BC returned to live there, the city was a small one; it is not even clear whether it was the capital of the province or subordinate to Samaria.

The excitement over a more populous future is coloured by frustration that the city continued to be such a pale version of itself, compared to its glory days as Judah's capital, when merchants and ambassadors from across the world came to bargain and trade. It is also within a context in which a town of a few tens of thousands of people would have been considered large; Babylon, the largest city in the ancient world, had a population of perhaps only 200,000. This is a very different context than ours, in which overpopulation and exhaustion of the planet's resources are among the most pressing global issues.

Indeed, the joy with which both Jerusalem and Yahweh greet the new inhabitants stands as a condemnation of our own carelessness with the population of our great cities, many of whom are mired in poverty. The satiation celebrated in verse 11 is alien to the children who go hungry in our streets. In verse 9 Yahweh claims Zion's children as Yahweh's own creation and reminds us that neglect of God's creation is an offence against Yahweh.

6 Worshippers gathered from the nations

Isaiah 66:18–24

The final verses of the book of Isaiah extend its vision as far as the mind can conceive. The centrality of the temple in Jerusalem as a sign of Yahweh's presence is renewed, as the delivery of people from all nations to Jerusalem are likened to offerings (v. 20). That this is to be understood positively (rather than as some sort of divine demand for human sacrifice) is clear from the promise to ordain some of these foreigners as priests and Levites (v. 21). This vision thus revisits the radically inclusive vision of Yahweh's people presented in Isaiah 56, in which foreigners and eunuchs are promised a full welcome into Yahweh's temple (Isaiah 56:3–8), bringing these chapters' vision of Yahweh's restored community to a climactic conclusion.

Here, the most important criterion for inclusion in the 'the new heavens and the new earth' that Yahweh is creating is not ancestry but commitment to the worship of Yahweh – even if it means travelling across the face of the earth, in whatever conveyance one can find, to do it. This not a complete departure from earlier traditions, but it is a much greater emphasis. Deuteronomy presumes that most Israelites will be such by birth, while acknowledging the possibility that those not born into the community might join it (Deuteronomy 23:7–8); it also recognises the danger that those born into the community might abandon it (Deuteronomy 13). Ezekiel recognises a similar fluidity: those who claim Israelite heritage but fail to follow Yahweh steadfastly will be rejected (Ezekiel 8–11; 14).

Both of these envision such fluidity largely around the edges of the community; Isaiah 66 takes the possibility that foreigners will hear of and commit themselves to Yahweh to the most extreme conclusion. The present continuous verb – 'I am making' – to describe Yahweh's new creation signals that the transformation of the existing creation into a new creation is already taking place – it will not be delayed until the eschaton, nor has it already occurred.

The ordination of the people as priests and Levites and the affirmation that 'all humanity will come and worship me' (v. 23) signals the active involvement of the people in this process; this is not a summons to passivity.

Guidelines

These final chapters of the book of Isaiah revolve around a vision of Yahweh as the Lord of creation and the implications of this fact's full recognition. Before the exile, some Israelites had recognised Yahweh as the only God appropriate for them to worship (the pervasive admonishments to this effect suggest that it was not universally acknowledged). With the destruction of Jerusalem and the displacement of its inhabitants – some taken forcibly to Babylonia, some fleeing to the Transjordan or to Egypt, others forced to migrate within Judah's borders to survive – the people were scattered across the face of the earth. On this magnified international stage, replete with hundreds of competing deities, the Israelites were obliged to reckon with the power and reach of Yahweh.

The poetry of Isaiah 40—55 reflects a recognition of Yahweh's role as creator of the entire universe: Yahweh's power extended not merely to the Israelites and to their small kingdoms in the eastern Mediterranean, but over all the nations inhabiting all the earth. Isaiah 56—66 takes this theological revelation and expounds on its implications. Yahweh's invitation to membership in the community of Yahweh's chosen people is far more open than anyone had hitherto imagined: foreigners believed to be barred from Yahweh's innermost sanctuary are welcomed, and those whose physical limitations had been thought to exclude them from temple service are called to serve.

Yahweh's responsibility for all of creation also engenders an imperative among Yahweh's people to care for all of Yahweh's creatures: the homeless, the hungry, the poor, the neglected – all those who are marginalised by discrimination and miscarriages of justice. To serve Yahweh means to serve all whom Yahweh is gathering into the kingdom, pursuing lives of justice and righteousness that reflect Yahweh's character. Indeed, the new creation will not come about without our participation; we are called to orientate our every action towards Yahweh and towards the care of Yahweh's creation. In a twist of perfect justice, only those who fail to follow Yahweh's vision of a new creation characterised by radical inclusivity will be excluded from it.

FURTHER READING

Elizabeth R. Achtemeier, *The Community and Message of Isaiah 56—66: A theological commentary* (Augsburg, 1982).

C.L. Crouch, *Isaiah: An introduction and study guide* (Bloomsbury, 2021).

Jacob Stromberg, *An Introduction to the Study of Isaiah* (T&T Clark, 2011).

Louis Stulman and Hyun Chul Paul Kim, *You Are My People: An introduction to prophetic literature* (Abingdon, 2010).

H.G.M. Williamson, *Variations on a Theme: King, messiah and servant in the book of Isaiah* (Paternoster, 1998).

Honour and shame

Philip Grasham

This week our focus is 'honour and shame'. These are not exact opposites, but together they form one cultural and theological paradigm.

Western theology has emphasised the contrasting paradigm of innocence and guilt not just above but to the exclusion of honour and shame. This has done a disservice to believers appreciating a fully rounded biblical theology. How? Because it is indisputable that there is more said in the Bible about honour and shame than there is about innocence and guilt.

Jesus Christ was born, lived, taught and died in a culture which revolved around the principles of honour and shame. As theology and world view interact with each other, this means that both first-century Jewish theology and first-century Jewish world view built upon the honour and shame paradigm. Therefore, in 21st-century UK, a recognition of this paradigm would help people to preach, teach and share the gospel with people who hold this dissimilar mindset.

Western mission workers serving overseas have been grappling with the various dimensions of honour and shame for many years, but their home churches have rarely considered how these same dimensions could aid them in their own setting. This needs to be rectified, as it has become clear that a comprehension of honour and shame is increasingly significant in our multi-faith UK society.

It should be said that an understanding of honour and shame is not a magic key to unlock multiple cultural and theological conundrums. However, this missing dimension would help many people to better grasp the relational nature of God, especially the importance of adoption, reconciliation and restoration.

I pray that the Holy Spirit would lead you wherever these reflections may take you.

Unless otherwise stated, Bible quotations are taken from the NIV.

1 Ascribed honour

Psalm 113

When scholars use the terminology 'honour' and 'shame', what are they talking about? Honour concerns the significance or worth of individuals both in their own eyes and in the eyes of their community. It is a relational concept, with synonyms including approval, dignity, esteem, glory, reputation, respect, significance, status and value. Conversely, shame concerns a person's loss of reputation or status in their family or wider community, with synonyms including to deride, despise, exclude, insult, neglect, reject, scorn, stain and separate.

Those who hold an honour and shame mindset emphasise the collective and relational aspects of both culture and theology.

In today's reading, we discover some profound truths for honour and shame people. Our God is the king of the universe, worthy to be praised as the one 'exalted over all the nations' (v. 4). Yet he 'stoops down' (v. 6) – the Hebrew verb could just as easily be translated 'to become low' or even 'to be humbled'. God humbles himself to look at his creation – and what does he do? He lifts the poor and needy out of their dirt and filth (v. 7). This suggests that, specifically, these are the people he is looking for, and he raises them up and gives them seats of honour among the great and the good (v. 8). Imagine people sitting in rags on a refuse heap being taken from their poverty, clothed in fine linen and seated with royalty in a palace. What a wonderful truth! And for the childless woman – a point of great shame – the Lord gives a family and a home where there is joy and laughter (v. 9).

These psalms, and many others, show that whatever rejection and shame people have experienced, they can know that the glorious Lord accepts and restores them.

If this honour and shame framework is new to you, then the best place to start is in the Psalms. These beautiful yet sometimes shocking poems and songs are laden with the restoration of honour, reinstatement of reputation, deliverance from shame and humiliation of adversaries. Even in the lament and imprecatory psalms, we find the people of Israel crying out to be rescued from their shame and returned to covenantal honour. Yet, God's people also recognised the importance of continuing to honour the Lord by declaring his praises and singing about his salvation.

2 King David steals 'a little ewe lamb'

2 Samuel 12:1–14

In the life of David, son of Jesse, there are many examples of honour and shame.

In 2 Samuel 11, we have David's infamous infidelity. Occasionally, Bathsheba's character and conduct have been questioned, but the biblical text suggests she was someone who acted with humility and modesty, a loyal subject who would have been unable to say no to the order of the king. Bathsheba came from a distinguished family, with her husband counted among the king's best soldiers (2 Samuel 23:39). As such, she would have been a woman of status and rank who would not have let these community distinctions be lost easily. Also, the reason for her bathing was ritual cleansing and 'purifying herself from her monthly uncleanness' (2 Samuel 11:4). Plus, it should be said that the text says nothing about her being either naked or semi-naked.

So we come to today's reading and find Nathan beginning his parable by describing two main characters. This introduction established the social status of the two people: there is a rich man with many animals, showing his prominent position, which probably included providing for others, and a poor man with one little pet lamb who slept inside with his children. Nathan recounted that this rich host used his status to shamelessly steal from the poor man. The rich man is depicted as tight-fisted, inhospitable and selfish. The rich man's shameful act was disgraceful, and David agreed. Nathan explodes – you are the man!

David had despised the word of the Lord (v. 9); he had derided the covenantal pledge God had given to him to make him a great king. God had been faithful (v. 7) and, unlike the parabolic rich man, he was neither tight-fisted nor selfish and would have given David even more (v. 8). Once again, Nathan repeats the fact that David had despised God and disgraced himself (v. 10). In fact, he had shown 'utter contempt' for the Lord (v. 14). Consequently, because of David's arrogance, he will be humiliated. We have noted how important the family is in honour and shame societies, yet it will be through David's family that he will be dishonoured (v. 11).

We should note that, as we read through the Old Testament, not every story will use the words 'honour' and 'shame', yet the more we look, the more we will see that this is an essential theme for solid theological exegesis of the Bible's overall story.

3 The compassionate father (1)

Luke 15:11–21

We are going to spend the next two days looking at the parable of the prodigal son. We should recognise that the title normally given to this parable shows an unhelpful bias. Global South theologians understand that this parable is about the father, who willingly dishonours himself numerous times to reach out to both of his lost sons. Numerous scholars state that this parable is saturated with honour and shame. So, while this is such a familiar parable, we will see that there are some things which we, perhaps, continue to overlook.

First, contrary to popular belief, the younger son's shameful act was not so much in asking for his inheritance as much as in selling his inheritance and leaving his family behind. By doing so, he cut the family open, abandoned his household responsibilities and assumed he could survive without the love and support of his family. There is no doubt that the community would have been shocked and wondered: how could a son treat his family so shamefully? And how did the older son react? There is no mention, when, in reality, he should have been the one to step forward and mediate between the two sides.

Second, after the younger son 'came to his senses', our text specifically says that 'he got up and went to his father'. In honour and shame societies, an individual is always identified by his family, and the family is always the central point in a person's thinking. The text then implies that the father was watching the road and, although still a long way off, the father spotted that his son was coming back. The father 'was filled with compassion', hence my renaming of this parable's title. While the father could not see his son's face, and he had not heard his son's speech, his heart went out to his desperately missed son. As is well known, the father must have picked up his flowing robes, rejecting any sense of dignity and ran down the road. Why the haste? Apart from the obvious delight in seeing his son, the father wanted to reach his son before anyone else in the village saw him and reacted with hostility towards him (for all the pain and shame he had caused). The father's compassion overwhelming the younger son's sense of shame is palpable, and this increased as the father exuberantly embraced his errant son and kissed him. Jesus' first hearers must have been astonished at the father's actions. How about you?

4 The compassionate father (2)

As we continue from yesterday, there are two further points we can draw from this wonderful parable.

First, the father called for his servants to fetch three items – a robe, a ring and sandals. All three items demonstrated acceptance and the restoration of the younger son's status, both to the younger son and to the community. The father then called for the fattened calf to be killed and a celebration to be held. It is clear that choosing such a large animal indicated that the whole village was to be invited. Once again, it is significant that everyone needed to see that the father had accepted back his wayward child as an honoured son worthy of the family name. It has been noted that the father could have forgiven his son and then hired him as a paid servant or even an unpaid slave. However, while there was forgiveness, the father also reinstated him as his son and heir.

Second, the older son returned to the house and was perplexed as to why there were celebrations. On hearing that his rebellious brother was back and had been welcomed by his father with this feast, he refused to go in. Once more, the father went out to one of his sons. As the party's host, it was hugely inappropriate for him to leave, but, once again, the father bore that shame to engage with his older son. Almost immediately, he dishonoured his father by not giving any title or showing any respect (v. 29), and he proceeded to launch into an insolent tirade. Whatever else was going on, the older son clearly believed that this was not how the younger son should have been received home. In other words, this lavish honour to the shockingly dishonourable son was inconceivable. The father tenderly placated his older son with the remarkable words that 'everything I have is yours' (v. 31). We could say that the acceptance and forgiveness of the younger son did not diminish the father's commitment to the older son. So, in this parable, the father abandoned his honour and shamelessly embraced both sons. This parable is far more about the height of the father's compassion and love than the depth of the younger son's sin and shame. Hallelujah!

5 Jesus: the most honourable Saviour

Let's look at Jesus' passion through the lens of honour and shame. In our reading, what was, hopefully, unmistakeable was that Jesus was the most honourable person throughout the account of his arrest, trial, crucifixion and resurrection.

First, when the crowd arrived to arrest Jesus, it was Jesus himself who gave commands and controlled the situation. As the soldiers fell back, he continued to direct the proceedings, even taking time to instruct his disciples and reattach Malchus' ear. We must never forget that no one took Jesus' life from him; rather, he laid down his life for God's glory.

Second, the process of crucifixion was done in the most public way to cause the most dishonour: mocking, scourging, ridiculing, spitting, stripping naked and publicly executing. However, the Messiah endured these things and reversed their value. In other words, rather than Jesus being shamed, Jesus' honour was increased. The evidence for this is Christ's glorious resurrection. Philippians 2 is a key text, showing how Jesus brought honour to God through his obedience. He stepped down into humiliation and ignominy but was raised to renown and reputation. The resurrection is the great vindication that he who had been treated so shamefully was, in fact, the eternal Son of God, and the Father exalted him and bestowed on him glory and honour.

Third, because of the crucifixion, Jesus defeated shame alongside sin, the Satan and death. This means that shame, as well as fear and guilt, has no place or power over humanity. Jesus scorned the shame of the cross (Hebrews 12:2), demolishing its insidious influence and deposing its debilitating impact. At the same time, Christ's cross was a public shaming of the Satan and his forces (Colossians 2:15). The Great Shamer has been defeated, denounced and put on display for all to see him for who he is.

For anyone with an honour and shame perspective, all of this is radical and liberating good news!

Yet, I wonder how many times our gospel presentations focus on innocence and guilt which, as one author writes, makes 'it appear that God is a God of law before he is a God of love'. For our friends, neighbours and even church people, we need to share a message of Christ who invites people to take his name and become members of his family. May we rejoice that our Father gives us a new status as his adopted sons and daughters.

6 The rupture of *koinonia*

Romans 3:21–31

I assume that most people's go-to biblical book on innocence and guilt would be Paul's letter to the Romans. Therefore, it can come as something of a shock when we realise that, according to the NIV, the words 'innocent' and 'innocence' appear just once, while the words 'guilt' and guilty' do not appear at all. Conversely, the word 'honour' can be found four times and the word 'shame' appears five times. Is it possible that western theology's stress on innocence and guilt has been too robust?

Good hermeneutics show us the cultural environment of the first century. We discover a time steeped in the values of honour and shame. Accordingly, present-day cultures, with the same perspective, can help us to understand this Pauline letter. One Filipina social anthropologist said: 'An explanation of sin should not focus on the "breaching of rules" so much as the "rupture of *koinonia*"' (Melba Padilla Maggay, *Transforming Society*, Wipf and Stock, 1996).

Verse 23 shows that 'all have sinned' – the context shows that this is both Jews and Gentiles rather than every individual. They are dishonourable because they have not properly honoured God but missed the covenantal purpose of glorifying him. Both Jews and Gentiles have shamed God's name through disgrace and disloyalty. Jesus did not fall short of the glory of God, but in his death and resurrection he both honoured God in our place and bore our sin. The sinner's shame is eradicated and a new status of honour is conferred in Christ.

As with Maggay's observation above, sin is not simply a violation against God's law but a diminishment of God's glory. Because we turn our backs on the creator and the Saviour of the world, we spoil his image in us and bring dishonour to his name. This has far more to do with our identity than simply the wrongs we have committed. One author explains: 'Shame is ontological while guilt is functional' (Mark Stibbe, *My Father's Tears: The cross and the Father's love*, SPCK, 2014). In other words, the first focuses on our sense of who we are, while the second focuses on what we have done. Sin, when it is only defined as 'missing the mark', is incomprehensible to people who hold an honour and shame world view. However, if sin is defined as a betrayal of God's love and an antisocial act against others, this concept is understood instantly.

Guidelines

These biblical truths of honour and shame need to be shared from all platforms and pulpits. I am not suggesting that guilt be excluded, but that the current imbalance be addressed. Both the honourable and judicial aspects of the atonement can be found in the scriptures. Thus, in the parable we have considered this week, the younger son declares both guilt and shame, 'Father, I have sinned against heaven and against you [guilt]. I am no longer worthy to be called your son [shame]' (Luke 15:21).

Jesus repeatedly chose to go to people of shame. He honoured the shamed every time he sat and ate with them. Such acceptance by a rabbi to these men and women of disrepute must have been shocking. Undoubtedly, Jesus' ease and enjoyment of such people sets an example that stands the test of time.

Consequently, we must become people who make time for the disgraced, sit with the rejected and offer compassion to the shamed. We should promote a message that reveals that the most honourable Lord Jesus knows all about shame and has destroyed the burden of shame.

A 'complete' gospel presentation challenges our society's perceptions of identity and worth. To those who struggle with these things, Jesus stretches out his hand and offers life, meaning and wholeness without embarrassment, exclusion or reproach.

For those who believe and receive the truth of the Messiah, we are given position and status. Because of Christ, we can hold our heads high in the face of our past, present and future. Ephesians 2:5–6 tells us that God made us alive with Christ, raised us up with Christ and seated us with him in the heavenly realms in Christ. What an honour!

FURTHER READING

David A. deSilva, *Honor, Patronage, Kinship and Purity: Unlocking New Testament culture* (InterVarsity Press, 2000).

John A. Forrester, *Grace for Shame: The forgotten gospel* (Pastor's Attic Press, 2010).

Robin Stockitt, *Restoring the Shamed: Towards a theology of shame* (Cascade Books, 2012).

Edward T. Welch, *Shame Interrupted: How God lifts the pain of worthlessness and rejection* (New Growth Press, 2012).

Jackson Wu, *Reading Romans with Eastern Eyes: Honor and shame in Paul's message and mission* (IVP Academic, 2019).

1 Corinthians

Nigel G. Wright

If, as has been argued, human beings are God's most problematic creatures then similarly the Corinthians were Paul's most problematic church. Founded in about AD48 by Paul himself with the active assistance of Priscilla and Aquila, and then of Timothy and Silas (Acts 18), Paul fairly saw himself as the church's father (4:15), with all the attendant joys and anxieties. Headaches there were aplenty (as we shall see), and he had to work hard to keep the church heading in the right direction. As he was writing from Ephesus a few years later, communication was not always easy. Hurts and misunderstandings crept in, as demonstrated by the way a previous letter had been misinterpreted (5:9–10) – and all this before Twitter and Instagram had been invented! At the same time, the letter contains some of the most sublime writing of which humans are capable, and chapter 13, the hymn to love, is surely near the top of the list.

If the following studies were to have a title, 'Grace and gremlins' might prove appropriate. God's grace, God's overflowing mercy, forgiveness and generosity, is mentioned at the beginning and the end of the letter (1:3; 16:23) and appears like a thread all the way through. It is no surprise therefore that the letter has its attractions for 'charismatics' (*charis* means 'grace') and their worship. In fact, all of us, as recipients of God's gracious gift of God's Spirit, are charismatics. We are graced.

What about the gremlins? Gremlins belong to folklore as mischievous creatures that get inside machines (computers?) and disrupt their working. Paul's apostolic task was to sort out the gremlins in Corinth. The idea is figurative, but the problems were real. They belong to fallen human nature. They are also found in today's church, so if we think we are standing firm we should be careful we do not fall (10:12).

Unless otherwise stated, Bible quotations are taken from the NIV.

1 Overflowing grace, potential problem

1 Corinthians 1:1–17

The Corinthian church had had a powerful induction into the growing company of those who 'call on the name of our Lord Jesus Christ'. Their conversion to Christ was real. They were unambiguously part of God's holy people (vv. 2, 9). What a great thing to be, then and now! But more than this, Paul gives thanks because the grace of God has made them extraordinarily rich in spiritual things: gifted, eloquent and informed (vv. 4–6). They are a stellar community in Christ, and Paul has great hope for them because they are eager, expectant and firm in faith. He also knows that it is not just beginnings that count but endurance and perseverance to the end (v. 8). This is a great picture of a youthful and enthusiastic church. If these verses were read as a call to worship in any church service, they would make us feel good about our calling – and that is Paul's intention.

Yet Paul quickly senses the beginnings of a problem. By some means people 'from Chloe's household' (v. 11) had communicated on quarrels that if unchallenged could become factions when unity and a common mind were imperative (v. 10). As their spiritual father, Paul hated squabbling. Humans (even regenerate ones) typically find it easy to fall out with each other. Here the divisions were connected with who may have baptised new believers on their conversion. We know that Apollos, a highly attractive and eloquent speaker, had followed Paul in Corinth (16:12; Acts 19:1), and that Cephas (Peter) and his wife were known there, probably having visited (9:5). These were figures of great prestige. Seemingly, immature believers were boosting themselves and dividing (perhaps into different house churches) according to who had baptised them. For that reason, and not because he devalues baptism, Paul minimises baptism in contrast with the power of the cross that ought to be a focus of unity (v. 17).

We boost our own egos when we divisively attach ourselves to 'celebrities'. It may not be their fault but that of those who seek a reflected glory. Even those who identified with Christ could have been at fault (v. 12). He is, of course, the only 'celebrity' we should attach ourselves to, but on this occasion it looks like a self-regarding claim to superiority rather than a humble magnifying of his overflowing grace. Grace inspires a cooperative not a competitive spirit.

2 Changing lenses

The constant temptation to boost our egos because of who or what we know leads Paul to address the question of boasting: 'Let the one who boasts boast in the Lord' (v. 31). For the Christian the primary reference point for the good and godly life is Christ himself. Christians should not 'get with the programme' of fashionable 'wisdom'. The cross has given us a different way of thinking and acting. And it's good to be different.

According to standard ways of thinking, the cross, after all, does not make sense. The idea that the God of glory should display divine power through a shameful instrument of torture, and there encounter lost creatures for their salvation, is not an idea we would invent. From a traditional Jewish (or indeed Islamic) point of view, it might be thought to compromise the glory of God and so be an offence. From a philosophical Greek perspective, it is not something that can be deduced from first principles and so is incoherent (v. 23). Yet paradoxically, those who believe in it have found the cross to have saving power (v. 21). God graciously meets us there. It unapologetically overturns human wisdom. Those who reject it consider it foolish. Those who accept it celebrate it and live in its power.

Such thoughts prepare us for equally radical ideas about the church. God does not call us because of our fine qualities or because we have 'made it'. God prefers the lowly, the despised, the have-nots, the are-nots (v. 28). This is how God chose and called Israel in times past (Deuteronomy 7:7). It is to show that 'this all-surpassing power is from God and not from us' (2 Corinthians 4:7).

To 'boast in the Lord' means to make much not of ourselves but of the Christ who is God's supreme coming among us, Immanuel. He is 'our righteousness, holiness and redemption' (v. 30). This leaves no room for self-aggrandisement. Nor does it allow for any personality cults or hero-worship, even of Christian leaders who are simply servants, however grateful we should be to them (3:5).

Sometimes in the church's history there have been divisive issues that really mattered – both then and now. Sadly, however, much of our factionalism has been personality-based, an arrogant seeking for advantage. This is shameful, and we should play no part in it.

2–8 August   105

3 Christ and the Spirit

1 Corinthians 2

Having boasted about all God gives to us in Christ (1:30) and made clear his own exclusive attachment to Christ in his ministry (v. 2), Paul makes much room in these verses for the Spirit (eleven mentions in sixteen verses). There is no tension here. Christ and the Spirit are distinct but inseparable. Through the Spirit the wisdom dwelling in Christ is imparted to us. The Spirit is the continuing presence of the risen Lord in the Christian community. Paul's self-confessed weakness and vulnerability and his self-perceived lack of eloquence (vv. 3–4) were the very platform through which God's power was experienced through the Spirit (v. 5). His self-effacing approach gives God the glory and undercuts any temptation to hero-worship. He is reinforcing what he has already said about celebrities (1:12–13) and what he will go on to say again (3:4). We should take note.

It is often pointed out that the word 'Trinity' does not occur in the New Testament. This is quite right. However, it is by any standard clear that the first Christians experienced God as Father, Son and Spirit, as is shown by these and many other verses. The word 'Trinity' may not appear, but the realities it points to certainly do. There is a shape to Christian experience, and it is threefold. Through Christ we have received the Spirit from God (v. 12). The gospel is not just about words but words empowered by the Spirit that have life-changing impact (vv. 4–5). Paul was so confident of divine inspiration that even the words he used in preaching and teaching were not his own invention but the gift of God (v. 13). This is one very good reason for paying careful attention to what Paul had to say, and by extension to all the scriptures (2 Timothy 3:16).

God's Spirit figures a great deal in this letter. All the evidence makes it clear that this church was living in a powerful dynamic of spiritual energy, one that went beyond what can be considered 'normal'. It set the community of the Spirit apart from everybody else (vv. 12, 14). Is there a temptation to feel superior? Yet verses 15–16 are not a licence to 'stand in judgement' on others but to discern things in spiritual perspective, to have the mind of Christ, which is humble (Philippians 2:5–11) and, like Paul, self-effacing. Christ is all.

4 All things are yours

1 Corinthians 3

Martin Luther penned the following words: 'A Christian is an utterly free man, lord of all, subject to none. A Christian is an utterly dutiful man, servant of all, subject to all.' We should overlook the gender-specific language characteristic of a former age and try to deal with the paradox. Being subject to Christ alone, Christians are fundamentally and inwardly free from any earthly power. For the same reason, they see themselves as servants of all, freely willing to prefer others to themselves. It is something along these lines that Paul intends when he affirms in verse 21 that 'all things are yours'. What exactly does he mean?

For a start, he is affirming that believers do not 'belong' to any of their leaders – this is not what baptism means. The freedom that comes in Christ is from all forms of political, personal, ideological or religious domination. To imagine otherwise is immaturity (vv. 1–3). Christ alone is Lord. We are baptised in *his* name. This says a lot about what churches are supposed to be – free communities that have broken with domination systems in order to belong to Christ alone. No one should take that freedom away (Galatians 5:1). And to serve Christ is perfect freedom. None of this is to denigrate the gift and calling of leadership but to see it in true perspective. Leaders are servants (v. 5). If the church is a temple (vv. 16–17), then Paul helped to lay the foundation. But the real foundation is Christ (v. 11). Others have shared in the sacred task and helped to build, but they are still only fellow workers. If the church is a field, the planting and the watering all have to be done. But the growth is given by God. Without God's grace, there is nothing doing (v. 7). So focus on God, not the servants.

So how are 'all things yours'? All things come as gracious gift from God. Because Christ belongs to God and we belong to Christ, everything that is God's and Christ's is therefore ours to share. Every good gift comes from God. No good thing is withheld from us. Wherever we find that which is good and holy in the world or the church, we may claim it as our own. There are no quotas or restrictions. Could there be a more expansive, generous, hopeful, inspiring vision? Such is the kindness of a God whose love endures forever.

5 Servants and stewards

To describe this chapter as biting satire would not be far off the mark. Paul is incensed by the arrogance shown by some in the Corinthian congregation (v. 19). Some years ago, the concept of 'super-spirituality' emerged in the church – boasting of spiritual experience for the sake of personal ego. It was rife in Corinth. There were those who bigged themselves up by believing themselves superior to others, either because of which leaders they claimed to follow (v. 6) or which gifts they thought they had been given (chapter 12). In Christ we have indeed been given everything (3:21). But in the present age we have not yet inherited all that is in him. There is much that awaits the full and final coming of God's kingdom. Some were (are?) guilty of what is called 'over-realised eschatology', the triumphalist assumption that everything is available now and we are outstanding examples of it (v. 8)! Paul refutes this by referring to the contempt, deprivation and dishonour shown to the apostles themselves. Though they were foremost Christian leaders, they were treated as rubbish (v. 13). They were servants and stewards, not superstars (v. 1).

Verse 7 is not only a key to understanding this chapter, but it is also central for the whole of Christian belief and living. Everything we have we have received. This is true without exception. Whether it is life, strength, ability or wealth, it is all the gift of God in creation. And whether it is new birth, faith, spiritual gifts or calling, it is all the gift of God in redemption. They come to us from the Father, through the Son and by the Spirit, by grace which is undeserved. Boasting of personal superiority makes no sense, and those who think otherwise need to be taught the better way (v. 21).

Satire is a form of humour, and humour often works by bringing together thoughts, ideas or images that clash with each other or are incompatible. The love and grace of God in giving us all things (3:21) just does not square with the idea that we are self-made, self-creating beings. At all points, we are dependent recipients of grace. This insight is at the heart of the doctrine of election – God has taken the initiative in gathering us into fellowship with God's own self. As with Israel, 'it was because the Lord loved you' (Deuteronomy 7:8).

6 Discipline in the church

1 Corinthians 5

Paul is clear that his mandate as an apostle of Christ and as the spiritual father of the Corinthians does not extend beyond the Christian community (v. 12). The instructions he gave in a previous letter should not be understood that way. He is concerned with relations inside the believing community, not outside it (vv. 9–10). He is equally clear that within the church he does possess the authority to judge between right and wrong. Yet even here he respects the responsibility of the church to sort its own affairs, doing so with his moral authority and encouragement (v. 4). It takes some courage and skill to discipline 'in love and with a gentle spirit' (4:21), which is probably why most churches today avoid it lest they be accused of, or even guilty of, psychological abuse.

The case in point is surely extreme and impossible to condone. Not surprisingly, it is to do with sex, but of a kind even pagans would condemn. For a man to sleep with his father's wife (v. 1) suggests that the woman in question is not his mother but his stepmother, perhaps one who was much younger than his father (common in the day even for a first marriage). This is scandalous and casts the young church in a bad light in the eyes of outsiders. Even worse, if left unchecked it could corrupt the whole church, spreading like yeast through dough and compromising its holiness. Radical surgery is necessary to stop the infection. This means excluding the offender from the congregation (vv. 5, 13). The somewhat alarming language of verse 5, being handed over to Satan for the destruction of the flesh, means just that: having come out of the dominion of darkness he is to be returned to it. Yet even here the intention and hope is that through bodily exclusion 'his spirit might be saved'. If 2 Corinthians 2:5–11 refer to this same case, then discipline may indeed have achieved its intention.

Church discipline is not easy, but perhaps there is a way of thinking that can help us. Its primary intention is not to punish or exclude but to disciple and guide. Our attitude towards it can make all the difference. Exclusion is a serious matter. It should only become necessary when every other pastoral and spiritual avenue has been explored.

Guidelines

In the language of the Nicene Creed, Christians are said to believe in 'one, holy, catholic and apostolic church'. The word 'catholic' can be taken to mean both universal in nature and faithful to 'the faith that was once for all entrusted to God's holy people' (Jude 3); this is affirmed also by the word 'apostolic'. Such are the marks that are considered to characterise the true church. If so, the church in Corinth, significant though its experience of God's power certainly was, had some way to travel before it could qualify as a 'true' church. But then, where has the 'true' church ever really existed?

The faults we have uncovered in this church, and will do so again, differ little from what can be found in all churches at all times, our own included. Should we then despair of anything better? Can the church ever rise to meet the challenge of 'one, holy, catholic and apostolic'? Answer: only by God's grace. And yet God is faithful, persistent and sovereign. 'If God is for us, who can be against us?' (Romans 8:31). There is hope, but it is in God, not ourselves.

Two perspectives might inform us. The first is that although we currently fall short, we are also given a vision of a church that one day will indeed be one, holy, catholic and apostolic. That ultimate vision is found in Revelation 7:9: 'There before me was a great multitude that no one could count, from every nation, tribe, people and language, standing before the throne and before the Lamb.' How God's grace will bring the vision to pass is not known to us, but that God will do so is sure. We should ponder this from time to time.

The second perspective involves embracing the 'marks of the church' not as an achieved and invariable state but as a working agenda: it is what we are working towards, even if it is no easy task. It is therefore the responsibility of every follower of Christ and member of the church to promote unity, holiness of life, radical openness to all conditions and manner of people and apostolic faith (both preserving it and promoting it). Whatever we do that offends against the vision is sinful obstruction to the divine purpose. We can be part of the solution, not of the problem.

1 You were washed

1 Corinthians 6

Corinth was renowned for its culture, wealth and sexual promiscuity. The latter is reflected in verses 9–10. Reflecting the preoccupations of our present age, our eyes tend to be drawn to 'men who have sex with men', one of the few biblical references to same-sex practice. Paul apparently disapproves. But there are current debates about what exactly he was disapproving of. Was it casual and abusive sex? Or a reference to prostitution? Or would he also disapprove of faithful and bonded same-sex partnerships? For some, the answer is obvious one way or the other. What should be agreed upon is that these verses should not be 'weaponised' in order to attack people who are also objects of God's grace.

The important thing for Paul is not what these various people used to be but what they have now become. They have been washed from past sin. They have been set right with God and made holy (notice once more in verse 11 the Trinitarian dynamic). Each one has a testimony. These Corinthians are not what they should be, but neither are they what they once were; some of them have quite a way yet to travel. Paul singles out Christians who go to law against each other before pagan courts. The logic of this is absurd (vv. 2–4) and it signals defeat (v. 7)! This is no way to build harmonious community. It would be far better to allow oneself to be wronged than to wrong others! Wrongdoing does not prepare us for God's coming kingdom (v. 9).

Another sign of super-spiritual immaturity is touched on in verse 12. In time this will come to be called 'antinomianism' – the rejection of any form of law or guidance for the believer once 'saved': 'I have the right to do anything.' Grace does not mean we are free from any moral obligations; it means that we are enabled to do what is right, renouncing immoral behaviour for good, in order to be united to Christ, who empowers us to live a new life in love and holiness. We are now temples of God's Spirit, made for God's honour.

I am not what I should be. I am not what I want to be. But I am not what I was, and by the grace of God I am what I am.

John Newton

2 Marital relations

1 Corinthians 7:1–15, 32–40

A persistent myth about the apostle Paul is that he was a misogynist. Given more space, we could demonstrate why this is not true. We should at least remember that the remarkable Priscilla was a fellow-leader who helped Paul establish the church in Corinth (16:19). This long chapter points us in the right direction.

In the ancient world, the relation of husbands to their wives was one of domination: men had unilateral authority over their women, in the home and in society. In this chapter, Paul, if we follow him carefully in verses 1–7, couches everything in terms of mutuality and reciprocity: whatever he says to men he parallels with the same affirmation to women. For example, in verse 4, husbands have authority over the bodies of their wives, but so also women have authority over the bodies of their husbands. If they forego conjugal relations, it must be by 'mutual consent' (v. 5). This denotes equality and mutual consideration and is the proper model for marriage. In its time it was revolutionary. Later references to women in 1 Corinthians should be read in this light, as we shall argue.

In the rest of the chapter Paul labours to uphold the importance of marriage. It is significant that he draws upon the teaching of Jesus passed down to him (v. 10; see Matthew 5:32) but at the same time makes it clear that he himself has the authority to make judgements in areas where the teaching of Jesus had to be interpreted and applied (v. 12). He can do this because he has the Spirit of God (v. 40), who gives access to the mind of Christ (2:16). We are not apostles, but in our own way we have the capacity for moral discernment by the same means, though we need to be humble about it. We are not always right.

Paul discerns the need to uphold marriage and to avoid divorce, unless this becomes inevitable, as in the case where an unbelieving partner wishes to break the bond (v. 15). Being married to an unbeliever does not render a partner or their children 'unclean' or somehow illegitimate: they are all 'sanctified' by the believing partner and may come themselves to believe through their witness (v. 14). At the same time, Paul, unmarried himself, sees singleness as a holy estate with considerable spiritual advantages (vv. 32–35).

3 The robust conscience

Reading 1 Corinthians is like listening to one end of a telephone conversation. Paul is responding to questions posed to him and we have to work out what those questions and comments are from the way he responds. This is particularly difficult because the best Greek manuscripts we have contain no punctuation and are written in capitals with no spaces between the letters! Bible translations do their best by supplying punctuation, as here in verses 1 and 4. Paul is quoting back what has been either written or relayed to him. Characteristically he goes as far as he can to agree with what is said and then draws back from it in order to set it in a different or more insightful light. He thus mediates between different underlying concerns, like the ones in this passage.

A big issue for the first Christians was whether to eat meat sacrificed to idols. Most meat was slaughtered in this way. When social and business life involved eating together, whether to eat such meat was a matter of conscience. Those who had robust consciences could argue that idols are nothing and eating neither brings us near to God nor takes us away (vv. 4, 8), so what's the problem? Those with weak consciences (v. 12), perhaps converts from paganism or cautious Jewish believers used to taking care about table fellowship, felt it could be a compromise. If pressed upon them, it could push them out of the church and lead, in spiritual terms, to their destruction (v. 11). One senses that those of robust conscience are behaving in a high-handed or arrogant way, flaunting their freedom (v. 9) in a way that is not beneficial (6:12). Even though Paul probably agrees with them in principle, he does not approve of their aggressive attitude.

There is a saying: 'In essentials, unity; in non-essentials, diversity; in all things, charity.' This is Paul's policy (Romans 14:1–7). The key verse affirming that all things come from the Father through God's Son the mediator (v. 6) is a hugely world-affirming and positive place to start. Yet in the non-essentials he still highlights the importance of conscience: to do what conscience forbids is never the right policy. To expect others to act as though your conscience should be theirs is bullying, another gremlin in the Corinthian machine. It offends against the practice of mutual love.

4 Rights and responsibilities

Surprisingly, bullying even seems to be directed at Paul (v. 3), and this confirms the impression that some in Corinth are simply too big for their boots and are causing trouble. It is not unknown that some who have profound spiritual experiences begin to think too highly of themselves. This is clearly painful.

Paul's lifestyle comes in for criticism: allegedly he is in it for what he can gain. Paul brings several Old Testament examples to bear to show that he has a right to be supported in his ministry. Yet from the beginning he has forgone this right precisely in order to be blameless (v. 15). He is constrained to preach the gospel, and the reward is not money but the fulfilment of his calling (v. 18). Paul is utterly single-minded and undistracted. Unlike other apostles he has no wife to accompany him. His commitment is to singleness, and therefore celibacy, so that he can give himself more fully to the task (7:29–35). His policy is to reach everyone for Christ. Verses 19–23 are no indication that he lacks principles (some detractors may have accused him of this too) but that he has trained himself to understand the different worlds in which he operates so that he can adapt, presenting the gospel in the ways that can appeal to people in their particularity and differences. He was unbelievably successful in this, turning the world upside down, so it seemed (Acts 17:6, ESV).

Paul had his faults and could sometimes be angular (he could fall out with others, though usually when something important was at stake). But it is impossible not to be impressed by the personal self-discipline that he brings to his ministry (vv. 24–27). He regards himself as an athlete constantly keeping himself in condition, making every action count, not giving in to the sluggish tendencies of body or soul, and above all pursuing the crown that will last forever (v. 25). What a man! What an example! What an inspiration! What a price to pay.

Do any of us feel we can match Paul's sense of dedication? We have spouses and families, ties and obligations, livings to make and careers to build. We can still be stirred, goaded and galvanised into giving 'our utmost for God's highest', celebrating the fact that like Paul we are free (v. 19).

5 Christian integrity

1 Corinthians 10:1—11:1

Paul in chapter 8 has shown himself to be a libertarian, allowing people space to follow their consciences in disputable matters. At the same time, he has made it clear that if our own behaviour causes others to act against their consciences, we are acting wrongly. We must be circumspect. We are free but should hold back upon that freedom if we are likely to cause others to stumble. In 10:23–30 he repeats this argument and advice. It amounts to a positive celebration of God's good gifts combined with a warning always to pursue what is constructive and beneficial for others (10:23–24). We may not face the same issues as the Corinthians, but every generation of believers will have its own challenges, and we need the mind of Christ and the guidance of scripture to hold the balance between freedom and responsibility.

Paul's use of the Old Testament is indicative. In the history of Israel are warnings and examples aplenty from which to learn (10:11–20). We should not neglect them. They have a continuing purpose. As a well-educated Jew, Paul is steeped in the knowledge of the ancient Hebrew scriptures; yet as one who has encountered the risen Lord, he reads those scriptures in a distinctly Christian way. He finds Christ everywhere – a clear indication that he understands Christ to have been active in the world as the Word of God prior to his incarnation (10:4, 9). The primary lesson to be drawn is not to compromise the knowledge of God in Christ by deliberately joining ourselves to alien spiritual powers. We drink the cup of Christ, not that of demons (10:21). Christian freedom is not about compromise. We do everything we can to relate well to people, but we only do what brings glory to God (10:31–33).

One of the ways in which we may maintain our Christian integrity is through the sharing of bread and wine in the meal that Jesus instituted (10:21). If idolatry is about giving our ultimate allegiance to something that is not God, but rather has the status of a demon (10:20), then participating spiritually in the body and blood of Christ helps to maintain our communion with the one who keeps us from delusions and deceptions, Christ himself (10:16–17). Why neglect this means of grace? Why not rather live lives of wholehearted thanksgiving?

6 The table of the Lord

1 Corinthians 11:2–34

And so Paul's thoughts are led to Christian worship. Here is a passage about which arguments have raged and the logic of which is, in truth, not always easy to follow. This is compounded by the fact that we do not fully know what Paul means by 'head', nor what the context required, nor whether he is speaking of head-coverings or hair as a covering, nor what an accurate translation should be. Some have despaired of fathoming what is going on!

So, to cut a long story short, we take the view that 'head' should be taken as 'source' (as of, for example, the head of a river) rather than as 'rank' (as of, for instance, the head of an organisation). Paul is therefore speaking of mutual interdependence between male and female (v. 12), following the trajectory of chapter 7, rather than authority relations. Additionally, the issue is not to do with head-coverings but with the ways in which hair is worn. In context, a man or woman's hair could be worn in ways that indicated sexual availability, and this is what Paul considers inappropriate, particularly when praying or prophesying (vv. 4–5). Paul's overall concern therefore is with decency and propriety, as determined by bringing glory to God and by the customs of the local context. Freedom should not become licence.

Debates about male and female relationships should not divert us from what Paul goes on to say about a central act of Christian worship (v. 20). Here we find a form of words often described as 'the words of institution' of the Lord's Supper (vv. 23–26), the sharing of bread and wine to recall Jesus' sacrifice and as a means of participating in his saving death (10:16–17). These words go back to Jesus himself (e.g. Matthew 26:17–30). They have been carefully passed on, as Paul indicates in verse 23. The vast majority of Christians still observe the Lord's Supper, although under a diversity of names and through a variety of means ranging from the simplest to the most elaborate.

Paul's concern is that the true meaning of the Lord's Supper, being one body in Christ (10:17), should not be denied by selfish behaviour in the church. The rich should not shame the poor by eating without them. To 'discern the body of Christ' means eating in unity and mutual love (v. 33). The neglect of these virtues brings harm to Christ's body (v. 30).

Guidelines

There are many things in the New Testament world about which we wish we knew more. Who exactly was Apollos, and how did he come to learn the way of Christ independently (1:12; 3:4; Acts 18:24–28)? What must it have been like to be Peter's wife, how did she come to share his faith and how did she adapt to his apostolic lifestyle? What were the other apostles and their wives doing and did they get 'paid'? How many brothers did the Lord have exactly, how did they all come to believe and were they regarded as having the same authority as the apostles (9:5–6)? We might pick up some hints as to the answers both in the New Testament and outside it, but it would be fascinating to know much, much more. It is notable how many gaps there are in our knowledge.

One of the areas of ignorance concerns the church's gatherings for worship. In this regard we probably know more from 1 Corinthians than anywhere else. It can be reasonably conjectured that believers met for worship on the evening of the first day of the week (16:2). Morning worship only became normal in the second century; before then most would be working during the day. Gatherings would be in the homes of those who had the largest houses (16:19), presumably the wealthiest members. A full meal, or *agape*, would be involved, followed by bread and wine, and then by more formal preaching and teaching and the use of the kinds of charismatic gifts described in the chapters to follow. Paul's suggestion that some people should eat in their own homes beforehand (11:34) perhaps points to Communion becoming a separate and more ritualised meal. Yet we know little about who would preside at or lead worship. Worship as we experience it throughout the churches today seems somewhat different from what we read here. It is much more programmed. How much does this matter?

It *should* matter if we take our bearings from the New Testament. There are emerging principles on which to draw. In the next chapters Paul seeks not to stifle spontaneity but to give structure to active participation so as to make it more meaningful and helpful. If he writes little about who presides, he has much to say about the Holy Spirit who leads.

1 For the common good

1 Corinthians 12

If we take verse 7 as a key verse, we can enter into the spirit of this chapter: the Spirit of God, who enables us to cry, 'Jesus is Lord,' is made manifest through a variety of gifts, some of which are listed in verses 7–10, for the benefit of the congregation. This is seen as a sovereign, dynamic, mutually upbuilding and interdependent process in which we give glory to God and minister to each other. Worship is not something we generate so much as a way in which we enter into the life of God and are enabled to respond to God and each other. Once more, the idea of grace, or gift, is central – 'What do you have that you did not receive?' (4:7).

What is given takes varying forms. On a broader canvas there are gifts of specific people, such as apostles, prophets and teachers (v. 28). These are enabling and stabilising ministries in the church. There are gifts here that require the Spirit-enabled use of the intellect (Paul himself being the most obvious spiritual intellect of the early church). Yet most of the gifts mentioned in this chapter are of a more immediate kind and involve intuitive dimensions of the human person. Speaking in tongues is the stand-out example of this, but the point carries over into other gifts mentioned. Many western Christians tend to find these aspects of Christian experience strange because they go beyond the more rational and cautious spirituality we are used to. Yet they belong to original Christian experiences, and it is hard to exclude them without implying that the first Christians got things badly wrong.

High-octane Christian faith can be very exciting, but as noted its shadow side is 'super-spirituality'. Human self-regard can take hold of anything for unhelpful reasons. It is clear that this was happening in Corinth. Some, probably those displaying the most intuitive gifts, considered themselves superior to others (vv. 15–20). They boasted, and in the process they missed the whole point. Gifts were for the common good, not for vanity. They were intended to unify the body of Christ, not to divide it (vv. 12–14, 25). When sinful human beings seize hold of spiritual realities to exalt themselves rather than Jesus the Lord, they become guilty of a particularly distasteful and wicked form of pride. Let's not go there.

2 The pre-eminence of love

1 Corinthians 13

This is one of the truly great chapters of all human literature. Faith, hope and love are the three cardinal virtues, with love being pre-eminent. In this sense Christianity may be thought to have triumphed, that hardly anyone anywhere denies the beauty of love. However, to know what love really is and how to practise it is a massive challenge. Love is continually being put to the test. Our ability to pass that test is the measure of our integrity as followers of Jesus.

Is it significant that this chapter falls between two other chapters that deal with the practice of worship? When it comes to things that touch us deeply, we do not find it easy to bear with others who think and feel differently. This is still the case in a church where 'worship wars' are common, often revolving around preferred styles of music and liturgy, formal or informal. And often we do not even think to look to the New Testament for our models of worship but simply assume that the way we have always 'done it' is the way it should be done.

Paul is at pains to stress that everything will pass away and that only faith, hope and love will endure into eternity. He means that all those things about which we get so stirred up in this life are only of relative importance. It helps us to see things in the perspective of eternity. When he speaks of leaving the things of childhood behind, he does not mean that spiritual gifts are signs of immaturity, though they are certainly partial (vv. 9–11). Rather, he means that our attitude to them might be. When we prize them as of supreme importance and use them to compete, we behave like children and need to grow up.

Mature Christians have a robust *faith* in the living God, a faith that can weather disappointment and that is informed by God's wisdom. This faith gives purpose and meaning to the whole of life. It is shaped by a *hope* that looks into the future and knows that with God all manner of things will finally be well. It issues in a quality of *love* that has let go of self-importance and been set free to find fulfilment in giving to others. Like this chapter, it is beautiful. Love is supreme.

3 Order and passion in worship

1 Corinthians 14

Paul says nothing in this chapter to dampen the use of spiritual gifts – quite the opposite (vv. 1, 5, 18, 39). Since God is not a God of disorder, Paul does, however, stress the need for an orderly process (vv. 26–33, 40). The intention is to draw out the maximum benefit for everybody from the manifestations of the Spirit with a supreme stress on intelligible and upbuilding contributions (particularly verse 19). The more excellent way of love (12:31) demands that we build each other up rather than opt for personal satisfaction (vv. 2–5). Intuition and intelligibility belong together in a unique fusion, and neither quality should be despised.

Into this wise and constructive passage, however, a discordant note is inserted that is hard to ignore. Verses 34–35 apparently impose a prohibition on women speaking in church. Its presence here has compounded the idea that Paul was a misogynist, a distortion we have already challenged. It is widely considered that these verses are not original to Paul but have been copied into early manuscripts by a scribe who did not share Paul's consistently liberating approach. For a start, if the verses were removed the chapter would flow better (try it). Second, the 'law' (the Old Testament) does by no means enjoin silence on women at any point. Third, and most significantly, 11:5 has already endorsed women 'prophesying'. This very chapter is addressed to believers generally and encourages them to seek and employ spiritual gifts, apparently without regard to gender (vv. 1, 26, 39 – remember that when the New Testament uses the word 'brother', it does so in a gender-inclusive way, as was common practice in English until recently).

It is well-established that some modifications to what we believe to be the original text have crept into New Testament manuscripts in the early years. To identify and exclude these could suggest we are simply cutting out texts that we find inconvenient. On the other hand, to give scriptural authority to verses that do not properly belong there is itself profoundly unhelpful and unfortunate, causing problems and wrong turns that need not exist. Readers will wish to make up their own minds about these verses (in the recommended reading, the books by Bartlett and Hays will help). Those who seek to live authentically 'under the word' need to work hard to know what that word authentically is.

4 Fundamentals

1 Corinthians 15:1–34

Surprisingly, some Corinthians were even questioning such a fundamental conviction as Christ's resurrection. Paul takes them back to the basics (vv. 1–2). In doing so, he reveals so much. Verse 3 indicates what he himself had received at the time of his own dramatic conversion. He takes us back to within three or four years of Christ's resurrection in either AD30 or 33. This is the earliest of all accounts of the resurrection (earlier than those in the gospels), and it is solid. The use of Peter's nickname 'Cephas' reflects the Aramaic substratum of the resurrection traditions handed on from the beginning. It refers to repeated and diverse appearances by Christ to individuals who could be named, consulted and questioned. We know little about the appearance to the 500 (v. 6), regrettably. Paul does not mention the empty tomb, but then there is much that he does not mention (not least about Jesus), probably because it was already known and assumed by his hearers. His purpose is to ground Christ's resurrection unmistakably in history. He himself is a direct witness to the risen Christ (v. 8), so he refutes those who for some reason deny it (vv. 12–14). Verses 16–19 speak for themselves with a loud voice!

The resurrection is the very ground of our faith, without which there is nothing to hope for. Crucial to Paul's thinking, and influential ever since, is the polarity he sets up between Christ and Adam: in Adam (that is, in our shared, fallen condition) there is only death for us all, but in the risen Christ all can be made alive (v. 22). We are either defined by 'Adam' or redefined by Christ, and there seems to be no limit how far this new creation might reach. What a vision!

All of this is part of a divine purpose by which the risen Christ is the crucial new beginning that will lead steadily to the dismantling of evil, the death of death and the restoration of all things to God so that 'God may be all in all' (v. 28). The Corinthians had developed an idiosyncratic baptismal practice, perhaps of deceased converts who had missed out on baptism (v. 29). Without endorsing it, Paul points out how contradictory this practice would be were Christ not indeed risen. Christ is alive, and so we may risk all things for him (vv. 31–32).

5 Resurrection not resuscitation

Questions inevitably abound. Jesus was raised, not just resuscitated. The body of Jesus was not simply revived and restored to mortal, bodily existence, as was the case with those he himself raised, such as Lazarus. If this were so, his body would have needed to die again. Instead, his body was raised out of mortal existence and beyond the very possibility of death (Romans 6:9). To explain this, Paul uses several illustrations to argue that a seed is sown as one thing when it dies in the ground, but is raised as something else (vv. 35–38). There is a continuity and a discontinuity between one form of existence and the other. Christ's perishable body died but was raised as something imperishable. It was raised in glory and power as a spiritual body (vv. 42–44), something like a life-giving spirit or a 'heavenly man' (vv. 45–49). This is not a corpse being returned to life after catastrophic collapse, but something absolutely new, an eternal reality eclipsing a reality in time. The mortal is swallowed up by the immortal, raised to a higher power.

This opens up a whole new creation for Christ and a whole new phase in his ministry. He is no longer bound to Galilee, Judea or Jerusalem but is available for all people everywhere in the Spirit. What happened to him in resurrection will happen to us in the fullness of God's time; yet we feel ourselves on the verge of it (vv. 49, 51–52). We will all be changed. Yet the glorious Christ is still Jesus of Nazareth, the same yesterday, today and forever (Hebrews 13:8), the one whom we love as our brother and friend (Hebrews 2:11–12). Whereas in his earthly life the glory of God in him was concealed and hidden, only occasionally being glimpsed, now we behold his glory in its fullness, and as we gaze we become like him (2 Corinthians 3:17–18).

We speak here of something even Paul struggles to explain. He is dazzled. One perspective on it is that in the resurrection God's ultimate and future reality has appeared in time, giving us a glimpse of what one day will be reality for us and for all the world. There are times when the truth of God becomes a mystery to be adored, rather than a puzzle to be explained. We are at such a point.

6 Back to earth

After flying high, our final chapter brings us down to more familiar realities. Paul has for some time been building a relief fund (the world's first?) to help the impoverished believers in Jerusalem. The gathering of funds sets a good example both of organisation and of responsible management, as well as being a tangible expression of love across the barriers of geography and ethnicity.

Paul commonly ends his letters with personal news and greetings. These act as a reminder that he himself was highly dependent on his fellow-workers. This was true of his apostolic, church-initiating tasks but also of those times after Paul had moved on and the work needed consolidation and maintenance. Many of the names mentioned are not people we know, but we stand on their shoulders and probably would not be here were it not for such as they. We are also reminded that all Christian workers remain vulnerable human beings. Did Timothy suffer from timidity (vv. 10–11)? Did Paul find the glamorous Apollos a tad uncooperative at times (v. 12)? Did Paul get overwhelmed by the expectations upon him (vv. 5–9)? Aquila and Priscilla invariably appear in the New Testament as exemplary Christian leaders. Their position as relatively wealthy and competent business-people unselfishly dedicated to the work of the kingdom is an inspiration.

Given that the church in Corinth presented Paul with a number of severe difficulties (and more gremlins could be located in 2 Corinthians), it is tempting to ask how they were able to hold together and how it is that Paul persisted with them. One can only conclude that there was a high quality of spiritual life that outweighed the challenges, that they had a deep experience of God's grace and that the church was bound together and to Paul by sheer love. Love here should be seen as more than a benevolent attitude to each other, but as a deep and caring connectedness. If 1 Corinthians 13 sets this out in classic terms, this final chapter drives it home: 'Do everything in love' (v. 14); 'My love to all of you in Christ Jesus' (v. 24). Then there is the 'holy kiss' of verse 20, a physical expression of mutual affection and togetherness parallel to the hugs, handshakes and fist-bumps of other cultures. Christian community at its best is a miracle. Thanks be to God.

Guidelines

I listened to a mother describe a game she played with her children. They had to think of something, anything, that would make her stop loving them. Nothing they ever came up with would do it. Her love was unconditional, unshakable, irrevocable. At the same time, when the children crossed the boundaries she set of right and wrong, she was fierce, uncompromising, even judgemental. This sounds to me like a recipe for a healthy childhood.

This mother happened also to be a rabbi; in her motherhood she was reflecting the nature of God as 'our Father, our King', the God of everlasting love and holy rule: 'For the Lord your God is a consuming fire, a jealous God' (Deuteronomy 4:24). How different this is from the much-espoused maximally mellow God who is seemingly indifferent to our sins. Accept us in grace God certainly does, but not to overlook our faults. Nor does God leave us as we are. It is God's work to bring about transformation, to neutralise the gremlins that infest us, to cultivate the resurrection life within us.

In his dealings with the Corinthians, Paul shows himself to be a true apostle and a faithful father. He demonstrates the patient love that he so highly prizes but does not overlook those aspects of the early Corinthian community that are unacceptable. He confronts them and shows there is a better way. He affirms what is good when he can but does not hesitate to correct when he must. He is wise. None of us are so mature or so spiritual that we do not stand in need of both affirmation and correction.

The Corinthians were certainly problematic. This should not blind us to the excellence that we also find here: a spiritually rich and dynamic community in which gifts were being freely expressed. It requires a certain level of passionate spirituality for this to happen, and passion is what many churches lack. If we feel superior to the Corinthians, we might consider how they also judge us, perhaps revealing to us our coldness of heart and lack of spiritual energy. We may exceed them in certain respects, but not in all, and should humble ourselves that we may learn that 'a living dog is better than a dead lion' (Ecclesiastes 9:4, ESV). Think about it.

FURTHER READING

Andrew Bartlett, *Men and Women in Christ: Fresh light from the biblical texts* (IVP, 2019).

Richard B. Hays, *First Corinthians: A Bible commentary for teaching and preaching* (John Knox Press, 1997)

Nigel G. Wright, *God on the Inside: The Holy Spirit in holy scripture* (BRF, 2006).

Tom Wright, *Paul: A biography* (SPCK, 2018).

2 Kings 1—13

Alison Lo

The books of Kings cover more than 400 years of Israelite history, dividing it into three sections: the reign of David and Solomon (1 Kings 1—11); the divided monarchy of Israel and Judah (1 Kings 12—2 Kings 17); and the kingdom of Judah alone after the fall of Israel (2 Kings 18—25). It is noteworthy that the books are not all about kings and their times, but rather more about God and faithfulness to him.

These coming two weeks will focus on 2 Kings 1—13, which starts with the transition of mission from Elijah to his successor Elisha and ends with the death of Elisha. Thus this block of text highlights the prophetic activities of Elisha during the divided kingdom of Israel and Judah. The ministries of these two prophets are distinctly characterised by clusters of miracles, which serve as a witness to God's sovereignty and power contrasted with that of the false gods. Interestingly, Elisha's miracles bear some similarity to Elijah's.

We will discover that, like his predecessor, Elisha ministers to people from all walks of life, including the poor and needy, widows and children, wealthy people, national kings, fellow prophets, foreigners (kings, officials, commanders, troops) and so on. This reflects God's intervention through the prophet in all aspects of life, which involve social, political, economic, religious, national and international affairs. The kings of Judah and Israel are commented on according to the extent of their covenant loyalty to God and their royal responsibilities to the people. Despite the failure of the kings, God's grace and mercy prevail forever and he keeps his promise to their ancestors: the lamp of David never vanishes, even on the brink of extinction. As we will see, the text asserts that the rise and fall of powers are controlled by the God of all nations and all creation.

Unless otherwise stated, Bible quotations are from the NRSV.

1 Common failure

2 Kings 1

An ancient Chinese proverb states, 'Failure is the mother of success,' which means failure is the greatest teacher. 2 Kings 1 underscores that Ahaziah fails to learn from failures. He continues the worship of Baal, established by his father, Ahab (1 Kings 22:51–53). When Ahaziah injures himself after a fall, he sends messengers to Ekron to consult Baal-zebub (Baal the Fly) about the fate of his injury instead of turning to God (v. 2). It indicates that Ahaziah has not learnt from his father's defeat on Mount Carmel, where the prophets of Baal were killed by Elijah (1 Kings 18).

The threefold repetition of Elijah's message to the king highlights Ahaziah's relentless apostasy and foolish stubbornness. First, the same challenge is raised by Elijah three times: 'Is it because there is no God in Israel that you are going to inquire of Baal-zebub?' (vv. 3, 6, 16). Second, the death of Ahaziah is prophesied three times by the prophet: 'You shall not leave the bed to which you have gone, but you shall surely die' (vv. 4, 6, 16). The message from God does not change just because Ahaziah does not want to hear it the first time. Despite the attempt to change his destiny, the king dies according to the word of the Lord through Elijah (v. 17). After all, Ahaziah's continual failures to repent have cost him his life.

When Ahaziah sends out military forces to arrest Elijah (vv. 9–15), the prophet authenticates his identity as the man of God by asking God to send fire from heaven twice, which consumes 102 men (vv. 10, 12). Some people find this incident problematic. However, we should note that when God commands Elijah to intercept Ahaziah's messengers and deliver his message to the king, the word of God is clearly shown to the reader. By contrast, there is no sign of God's command at all in the matter of sending fire from heaven. Whereas he rebukes the king for not consulting the true God, Elijah actually acts in his own way here, without seeking God's will. The failures of both the king and prophet echo each other in an ironical way.

2 Elisha's darker side?

2 Kings 2 highlights the dramatic ascension of Elijah to heaven (vv. 1–18), and confirms Elisha's commission by demonstrating his miraculous healing of water (vv. 19–22) and the judgement upon the mockers (vv. 23–24). This incident is one of the most disturbing stories in the Old Testament and troubles many modern readers.

The small children mock Elisha with the nickname 'baldhead' (v. 23). Then Elisha curses them in the name of the Lord. Thereafter, two female bears appear to maul 42 youngsters to death (v. 24). There is no easy answer to this challenging text. To address the issue, let's think about why Elisha is taunted. In the previous chapter, Elijah is known as a hairy man (1:8), which drastically contrasts with Elisha as a bald man. Elisha's legitimacy and authority as a prophet is denied probably because the successor's baldness does not seem to look like his predecessor's hairiness outwardly. Elijah's ascension to heaven demonstrates his God-given power, which probably prompts the children to jeer at Elisha (literally in Hebrew), 'Go up, Baldhead! Go up, Baldhead!' The bald Elisha is challenged to ascend like his predecessor.

Elisha's revenge is often justified by the idea that to deny God's messenger is to deny his divine purpose and sovereignty, which is considered to be culpable. It is further defended by the assumption that divine power cannot be used independently of God's direct action: the judgement befallen upon the children is not so much about Elisha's power, but God's choice to bless or to curse. Is this truly the case? The silence of the text opens up an alternate possibility.

The context shows that Elisha is quite mindful of his power when he requested Elijah for a 'double portion' of his spirit before his ascension (v. 9), which is proved when he successfully divides the Jordan river and heals the water (vv. 13–14, 19–22). When Elisha's power does not receive respect, he loses his temper. Though Elisha's angry act has no comment, no sign of God's endorsement is seen either. The reader has to make sense of it.

3 An enigma

This chapter bears similarity with 1 Kings 22. In the face of Moab's rebellion, Jehoram son of Ahab seeks an alliance with the king of Judah, Jehoshaphat, to battle against the Moabites (vv. 5–7a). Similar to his response to Ahab, Jehoshaphat agrees to ally with Jehoram (v. 7b; compare 1 Kings 22:4). But unlike before, Jehoshaphat does not consult God's will on this matter (compare 1 Kings 22:5). On their march to Moab, Edom joins the allied forces.

There is no water after a week's expedition (vv. 8–9). This crisis prompts Jehoshaphat to appeal to prophetic counsel (v. 10), which is similar to 1 Kings 22:5. However, this is not out of true piety but desperate need. Two assurances of God's help are given by Elisha. First, water will be miraculously supplied out of the wadi without wind or rain (vv. 16–17). Second, they will be victorious in this battle (v. 18). Sure enough, the word of the Lord is accomplished. The Moabites mistake the reflection of the rising sun on the water for a stream of blood. They think it must have been caused by an internal fight between the allied forces (vv. 22–23). The carefree Moabites are slaughtered when they approach the Israelites' camp.

The total devastation drives the Moabite king Mesha to offer his firstborn son as a burnt offering to his god (v. 27a). The text ends without comment and explanation: 'And great wrath came upon Israel, so they withdrew from him and returned to their own land' (v. 27b). Does the fury come from Mesha's god (Chemosh) or Yahweh? Or is it Israel that expresses great wrath against Mesha? The Hebrew text is ambiguous, and the reader is left hanging without any resolution to the enigma.

As Elisha foretold, the Israelites must have conquered all the cities and totally devastated the land – destroying every good tree, all the springs and every arable field (v. 19). Such devastation caused by the Israelites actually violates the 'rules of war' given in Deuteronomy 20:19–20. Human excess and mercilessness cause humanitarian and environmental disasters. It may be that this is what triggered Yahweh's wrath, leading to the reversal of Israel's initial victory (vv. 16–24) to their final withdrawal from Moab (v. 27).

4 God's care for individual needs

2 Kings 4:1–37

2 Kings 4 highlights God's care for individual needs by describing four miracles that God works through Elisha. Interestingly, Elisha's first two miracles (vv. 1–37) echo Elijah's, so they appear to be two doublets.

Elisha provides the needs for a widow and her two children by multiplying oil, which is sold to pay off the debts inherited from her dead husband (vv. 1–7). According to the law, the creditor would have been entitled to seize the debtor's property and children if the debt were unpaid at his death (Exodus 21:7; Isaiah 50:1; Amos 2:6; 8:6; Micah 2:9; Nehemiah 5:3–5). This story echoes Elijah's provision for the widow of Zarephath (1 Kings 17:8–16).

In the second story, Elisha takes care of a wealthy woman in two ways. First, he heals her inability to conceive by foretelling the conception of a child within a year (vv. 8–17). When the child grows older, Elisha raises him from death (vv. 18–37). Elijah's deed in 1 Kings 17:17–24 closely parallels Elisha's miracle. Whereas Elijah raises the dead son of the widow of Zarephath by stretching himself on the child three times (1 Kings 17:21), Elisha revives the dead boy by lying on him, mouth on mouth, eyes on eyes and hands on hands, twice (vv. 34–35). The two doublets above demonstrate that Elisha and Elijah have the God-given ability to perform miracles.

It is noteworthy that the miracles are performed privately in these two episodes. According to Elisha's instruction, the widow shuts her door behind her when she pours oil into the vessels (vv. 4–5). When Elisha raises the dead boy, he performs it behind closed doors (v. 33). The performance of miracles calls for human faith. When Elisha asks the widow to borrow vessels from all her neighbours to hold oil, she shows her simple obedience to the prophet's word (v. 5). Despite her husband's objection, the wealthy woman sets her mind to requesting Elisha to revive her dead son (v. 23). Upon meeting Elisha, she vows not to return home without his company (v. 30). Her stubborn determination reveals her faith in Elisha's life-giving power from God.

5 A reversal of fates

This chapter is divided into two sections. The first episode recounts the healing of the Aramean general Naaman (5:1–19a; some translations of the Bible render 'Aram' as 'Syria'). The second story depicts the greed of Elisha's servant Gehazi (5:19b–27). These two characters form an ironic contrast, which makes the chapter a complete unit.

Heeding his Israelite slave girl, Naaman seeks Elisha's counsel as to how he can be cured of his leprosy (vv. 2–5). Though Elisha's instruction at first seems ridiculous to Naaman, he eventually listens to his servants and receives healing by dipping himself seven times in the Jordan (vv. 10–14). The restoration from his leprosy prompts this pagan general to worship Yahweh in preference to his national god Rimmon (vv. 15–19a).

Elisha refuses to accept a gift from Naaman as remuneration because he knows that healing comes from God (v. 16). But Elisha's servant Gehazi finds it a waste not to take something from Naaman (v. 20). He lies twice to cover up his greed. Chasing after Naaman, who is on his way back to Aram, Gehazi lies to Naaman that he is sent by Elisha to request a talent of silver and two changes of clothing (v. 22). Then Gehazi lies the second time when his master asks him where he has been (v. 25). His exploitation and dishonesty lead to God's affliction of leprosy upon him and his descendants (v. 27).

The juxtaposition of these two episodes creates a great sense of irony by contrasting the characters in the stories. The afflicted Gentile (outsider) is healed, whereas the opportunistic Israelite (insider) is afflicted. Naaman's humility and healing lead to his conversion to the only true God, whereas Gehazi's greed leads to his drifting away from the life-giving God. The young girl captured from Israel is used by God to bring salvation to the Gentile, while Gehazi's deed is driven by his selfish motives. Elisha serves people for no gain, whereas Gehazi seizes the opportunity to exploit. Sometimes God humbles us by achieving his plan in a way which seems to be stupid in human eyes. This chapter demonstrates the reversal of fates and ironic contrast between characters.

6 The spectrum of prophetic concerns

2 Kings 6:1–23

This passage recounts two narratives regarding Elisha's ministries (vv. 1–7, 8–23). In verses 1–7, the company of prophets decide to move to the Jordan because they find their meeting place too cramped. They cut down trees to build an improved house in the new location. When one is felling a log, his axe head, which was borrowed, falls into the water. An iron axe was very expensive in ancient days. Losing such a valuable tool might result in great debt. To meet the need of this devastated man, Elisha performs a miracle by making the iron float, which seemingly violates the rule of nature.

Whereas Elisha serves the ordinary people in verses 1–7, he gets involved in the political arena in verses 8–23. The latter passage brings out a strong sense of irony when comparing the behaviour of different characters. To soothe his servant's nerve, Elisha asks God to open his servant's eyes so that he may see God's horses and chariots of fire all around Elisha, which outnumber those of the enemy Aram (vv. 16–17). To protect Israel, God strikes the Aramean army with blindness at Elisha's request, which allows the prophet to lead them to Samaria. Then God opens their eyes on their arrival according to Elisha's request (vv. 18–20). The servant's blindness to sight ironically echoes the Aramean experience from sight to blindness to sight.

The Aramean king is repeatedly frustrated by vain raiding against Israel (vv. 8–10) due to Elisha's discernment. Instead of turning back, his stubborn aggression presses him to silence Elisha's prophecy by sending a huge army (vv. 11–14). Though Israel's king could destroy his enemy, he listens to Elisha's counsel, feeding the Aramean troops and sending them home. The listening ears of the king of Israel contrast with the stubbornness of the Aramean king. Through divine intervention, the prophet successfully brings peace when on the verge of warfare (vv. 21–23). Both Israel and the Aramean army receive protection because of Elisha. The prophet's ministry ranges from small matters (such as finding the lost axe head) to big issues (such as fostering international peace), in which everyone concerned benefits.

Guidelines

Elisha inherits not only the mission from Elijah, but also the power of performing miracles from his predecessor, which is vividly demonstrated in 2 Kings 1—6. These chapters raise some points for our reflection.

- When God calls his servants into ministry, he will certainly empower them to carry out that ministry even though not everyone is called to perform the kind of miracles Elijah and Elisha did. This gives us assurance of God's assistance no matter what lies ahead in our ministries. Pray that the global church might have a strong sense of security even in face of opposition, crisis, death threats and other hardship, as the two prophets experienced.

- Like his predecessor Elijah, Elisha serves a wide spectrum of people: from the marginalised to the most honourable, from the national to the international arena, from God-fearers to idol worshippers, and so on. It demonstrates to us a God who has all peoples in his heart. How does the church today reflect that, and where does it fail?

- The kings are supposed to represent God on earth, but repeatedly they lead their people astray, falling short of God's glory. Even the great prophets of God (e.g. Elijah and Elisha) show their darker side. By contrast, the faith of some marginal characters, like the slave girl and the widow, uplifts our spirit like a breath of fresh air. Where is the authentic voice of God being spoken in marginal places, and are we missing it?

1 The fulfilment of God's word

2 Kings 6:24—7:20

The Aramean siege of Samaria leads to a severe famine, in which people suffer from a severe famine and as a result stoop to the horrific depths of cannibalism (6:24–30). The Israelite king mourns, wearing sackcloth during this national crisis. However, instead of leading his people to seek God's deliverance, he shifts the blame to Elisha and God. He recognises that this trouble comes from the Lord (6:33). But the text does not mention why the king wants to kill Elisha (6:31–32). Looking back to the preceding chapters, it is probably because Elisha has treated Israelites' enemy well by healing Naaman's leprosy (2 Kings 5) and releasing the Aramean army after feeding them (6:8–23).

In contrast to other places, Elisha does not perform a miracle in this passage. Instead, the fulfilment of God's word is highlighted here. Confronting the angry king, Elisha prophesies that the price of food will come down by the next day at the gate of Samaria (7:1), which means that the famine will break. In response to the disbelief of the king's right-hand man, Elisha declares that he will see the food, but he will not eat any of it (7:2).

The four lepers, who are excluded from the city (see Leviticus 13:11, 46; Numbers 12:14–16), report to the city about all of the possessions left by the Aramean troops (7:9–10), which saves Samaria from starvation. The Aramean troops, who were able to paralyse Samaria, mistakenly imagined they heard the sound of an enormous army, and fled in fear (7:3–8). The four socially despised lepers become brave heroes, while the strong Aramean troops prove to be cowardly army deserters. What an absurd reality!

Fulfilling God's promise through Elisha's mouth, the price of food comes down the next day due to the amount of plunder left by the Aramean army (7:16). When the people rush to scramble for food, the commander is trampled to death at the city gate (7:17–20), which fulfils Elisha's second prophecy (7:2). The four lepers serve as the heralds of good news to fulfil God's prophecy. Once again, we see God using small characters, such as these four outcasts, to accomplish his divine plan.

2 An evil plot for God's purpose?

2 Kings 8:7–15

King Ben-hadad of Aram falls ill, so he sends his trusted commander Hazael to inquire of Elisha as to whether he will recover (vv. 7–8). Elisha tells Hazael to report to his king that will certainly recover (literally 'certainly live'), but informs him that the Lord has revealed the opposite (v. 10). The incident raises some intriguing questions.

Elisha is based in Israel. Why does he journey to Damascus, capital of Aram (v. 7)? As we have seen (6:31–32), there is little love lost between Elisha and the king of Israel, perhaps because of Elisha's favour towards Aram (2 Kings 5; 6:8–23). Here, Hazael describes Ben-hadad as Elisha's 'son' (v. 9), suggesting a close relationship between the two men. Perhaps Elisha is trying to escape the pursuit of Israel's king, just as Elijah fled from Jezebel's capture (1 Kings 19:15).

Then why does Elisha lie? To protect Elisha's integrity, the Hebrew scribes changed 'Go, say to him (לוֹ, pronounced 'lo'), "You will live,"' to 'Go, say, "You will not (אֹל, also pronounced 'lo') live."' One may speculate that telling the truth about Ben-hadad's pending death might jeopardise Elisha's relationship with the Aramean king and thus his own life. We don't know for sure the reason behind Elisha's lie, but it actually incites Hazael to assassinate Ben-hadad. The scripture does not shy away from revealing the prophet's flaw.

This passage has a close connection with 1 Kings 19:15, where God has given a mandate to Elijah to anoint Hazael as king over Aram. Now it is Elisha, who moves to complete the unfinished mission of his predecessor. After all, God's word prevails, even though it is not accomplished through Elijah. More amazingly, Hazael's evil plot is used by God to fulfil his plan, in which he will serve as God's instrument to punish Israel in the near future. The rise and fall of powers reveal God's sovereignty. He is able to use anyone, whether good or bad, to serve his purpose.

3 Divine retribution

Elijah was commanded to anoint Jehu as king over Israel (1 Kings 19:16), but this task is not accomplished until Elisha appoints a young prophet to fulfil this mission (9:1–13). God raises up Jehu to avenge the blood of Naboth, who was killed by Ahab for not giving up his vineyard to the king. At that time, God declared that Ahab's house would be destroyed, especially Jezebel (1 Kings 21:21–24), who initiated the evil plot to pervert justice on behalf of Ahab (1 Kings 21:8–16).

This passage is full of the smell of blood, but we must notice some important details. Jehu kills Ahab's son Joram at the property of Naboth the Jezreelite (vv. 21–24). Not content with conducting a coup in the northern nation, Jehu also murders King Ahaziah of Judah, whose mother Athaliah is the daughter of Ahab and presumably Jezebel (vv. 27–28; 1 Kings 21:21–24). Then Jehu commands the eunuchs to throw Jezebel out of the window (v. 33). When they go to bury her, only the skull, the feet and the palms of her hands are found as the dogs have eaten her body, which vividly fulfils the word of the Lord through Elijah (vv. 35–37; 1 Kings 21:23). In addition, 70 sons of Ahab, anyone related to them, and all Baal worshippers are executed by Jehu (2 Kings 10).

Looking at the scene of this bloodbath, one has to question how Jehu's brutal onslaught can be justified, particularly since Ahab had already died in battle. We may find it uncomfortable when Jehu is commended for carrying out what God considers right (10:30). An alternative perspective is offered by the prophet Hosea, who names his son in memory of this moment: 'Name him Jezreel; for in a little while I will punish the house of Jehu for the blood of Jezreel, and I will put an end to the kingdom of the house of Israel' (Hosea 1:4). This verdict suggests that Jehu has overdone executing retaliation on behalf of God. Perhaps this is why his kingdom will only last till the fourth generation (10:30).

136   30 August–5 September

4 Jehoiada's contribution

2 Kings 11

This chapter resonates with 2 Kings 9—10 in many ways. As Jezebel was to Israel, Athaliah is to Judah. After her son Ahaziah was killed by Jehu (9:27), the Queen Mother Athaliah, the daughter of Ahab and presumably Jezebel, assumes the throne herself and attempts to annihilate the line of David in Judah. But Ahaziah's sister Jehosheba hides Ahaziah's heir, the infant Joash (Jehoash), in the temple (vv. 1–3), where her husband, the high priest Jehoiada (compare 2 Chronicles 22:11), protects the young prince with intense security (vv. 4–11).

When Joash is seven years old, Jehoiada contrives to crown him as king and execute Athaliah (vv. 12–16). The lamp of David is preserved in Judah according to God's promise (8:19). Like Jezebel, Athaliah's wickedness and brutality lead to her dreadful death in the end.

The royal intermarriage with the house of Ahab has led to prevalent worship of Baal in Judah. Like Jehu, who purged the Baal influence in Israel, Jehoiada acts in Judah to destroy Baal's temple, altars and images, and kills a Baal priest, Mattan (v. 18). But unlike Jehu, who took no care to follow the law of the Lord with all his heart and never turned away from the sins of Jeroboam (10:31), Jehoiada seeks to restore Yahwism by covenant renewal in Judah (v. 17).

Jehoiada's acts of restoration are well received by the people in Judah. That is why a joyful and quiet atmosphere is reflected in the conclusion of this chapter: 'So all the people of the land rejoiced; and the city was quiet after Athaliah had been killed with the sword at the king's house' (v. 20). It lays a strong foundation for Joash's reform in the next chapter.

5 The ambiguity of Joash's story

2 Kings 12

This chapter highlights the deeds of King Joash during his reign in Judah, which amount to a mixed picture. Following the instruction of the high priest Jehoiada, he takes the initiative to renovate the temple. But though he is commended by God for this, he is criticised for failing to remove the high places, which are the local sanctuaries for unauthorised worship (vv. 2–3).

Joash summons the priests to collect money from the census taxes (Exodus 30:11–16) and voluntary offerings (Leviticus 27:1–8) for the temple restoration and to oversee the project (vv. 4–5, 9–16). He also takes over the priests' oversight of the temple maintenance when they fail to get the temple repaired over two decades (v. 6).

But then, threatened by Aramean attack, Joash gives Hazael king of Aram all the temple treasury dedicated by his predecessors in order to buy him off (vv. 17–18). Ironically, Joash at first sets his mind to restore the temple, but in the end he robs it. The chapter ends on a tragic note as Joash is murdered by his officials (vv. 19–21). As an infant Joash's life was preserved as the survivor of the Davidic line, but now he dies dreadfully.

The story of Joash reflects a certain degree of ambiguity. The stripping of the temple treasury is not denounced, and the assassination of Joash is not explained in this passage. Elsewhere, the Chronicler points out that Joash does right when Jehoiada is alive (2 Chronicles 24:2), but that his reign is marred by covenant failure, idolatry and hostility between Joash and the priests after Jehoiada dies (2 Chronicles 24:17–22). Zechariah, the son of Jehoiada, publicly rebukes Joash, who thereafter stones the priest to death, triggering discontent and conspiracy against him in the nation. The Chronicler remarks that the apostasy of Joash leads to domination by the Arameans and his assassination by his own servants (2 Chronicles 24:23–25).

6 The death of Elisha

2 Kings 13

The opening reports (vv. 1–9, 10–13) and closing reports (vv. 22–23, 24–25) on Jehoahaz and Jehoash (the second and third kings in the line of Jehu, respectively) resonate with each other.

In the opening reports, both Jehoahaz and Joash are described as kings who did evil in the sight of God and followed the sins of Jeroboam, leading Israel away from God (vv. 2, 11). Concerning Jehoahaz, the Aramean oppression and God's deliverance from Aram relate to his fidelity to God, or otherwise (vv. 2–7). In the brief report on Joash, the mention of his fight with King Amaziah of Judah (v. 12) will be followed up in 14:8–14.

The accounts of both kings conclude on a note of grace. King Hazael of Aram oppresses Israel during Jehoahaz's reign. But God is gracious to the Israelites because of his covenant with Abraham, Isaac and Jacob (vv. 22–23).

As for Joash, he three times defeats Ben-hadad son of Hazael and recovers towns of Israel from Aram (vv. 24–25).

The death of Elisha lies in the centre of this sandwich structure (vv. 14–21) and contains some mysterious features. Knowing that Elisha is fatally ill, Joash goes to visit the prophet. The king is devastated and frightened of facing the future without the presence and power of Elisha after his death (v. 14). The prophet then offers Joash two signs for assurance that God will give him victory over Aram. However, the victory will be limited because of the king's failure to strike the ground repeatedly in what sounds very much like 'sympathetic magic' (v. 18). After Elisha's death, a corpse's body is revitalised by touching Elisha's bones (vv. 20–21), recalling one last time the power of God at work in both the life and death of the prophet. This small and puzzling detail calls to the mind of the Christian reader a similar, but much more dramatic, event at the death of Jesus (Matthew 27:52).

Guidelines

Fulfilling God's word to Elijah, 2 Kings 6:24—13:25 accounts for how Jehu and Hazael are anointed as kings over Israel and Aram, respectively, and how these two kings serve as God's instruments in Israelite history.

- This section bears witness for us to the power of God's word. Though sometimes it may not be fulfilled immediately, his promise will never fail. How does this speak to us today of the privileges and responsibilities of reading, studying, preaching and ministering his word?

- These chapters of 2 Kings present a challenging perspective on the justice of God. Jehu's purge is described as pleasing to God, but, as we saw, the prophet Hosea later condemns it. The slaughter of the sons and grandsons of Ahab might seem (to the modern reader, at least) unfair as punishment for the sins of their forbear. Rather than dismiss these narratives as unfaithful witnesses or uncritically accepting everything that we read, such tensions call us to engage more deeply, both with the text and with our own preconceptions. How is God's justice seen here? When is it deferred, and why? To what extent does our modern individualism clash with the ancient world view? What is God calling us to do?

- Hazael comes to power in Aram by assassinating King Ben-hadad of Aram. The reign of Hazael – pagan, murderous, ambitious – is used by God to fulfil his plan to punish Israel for their covenant disloyalty. We see a similar pattern later, when Babylon, God's instrument of judgement, is also subject to God's judgement for their misdeeds. How do these stories invite us to reflect, and act, when we read the newspapers in our own day?

FURTHER READING

Walter Brueggemann, *1 and 2 Kings* (Smyth and Helwys, 2000).

Gina Hens-Piazza, *1—2 Kings* (Abingdon, 2006).

T.R. Hobbs, *2 Kings* (Word Books, 1985).

August H. Konkel, *1 and 2 Kings* (Zondervan, 2006).

Helen Paynter, *The Strange World of Elijah and Elisha* (Grove, 2019).

Choon-Leong Seow, 'The First and Second Books of Kings' in *The New Interpreter's Bible: A commentary in twelve volumes*, vol. III (Abingdon, 1999), 3:1–295.

Marvin A. Sweeney, *I and II Kings: A commentary* (Westminster John Knox Press, 2007).

Become a Friend of BRF
and give regularly
to support our ministry

We help people of all ages to grow in faith

We encourage and support individual Christians and churches as they serve and resource the changing spiritual needs of communities today.

Through **Anna Chaplaincy**
we're enabling churches to provide spiritual care to older people

Through **Living Faith**
we're nurturing faith and resourcing life-long discipleship

Through **Messy Church**
we're helping churches to reach out to families

Through **Parenting for Faith**
we're supporting parents as they raise their children in the Christian faith

Our ministry is only possible because of the generous support of individuals, churches, trusts and gifts in wills.

As we look to the future and make plans, **regular donations make a huge difference** in ensuring we can both start and finish projects well.

By becoming a Friend of BRF and giving regularly to our ministry you are partnering with us in the gospel and helping change lives.

How your gift makes a difference

£2
a month

Helps us to develop **Living Faith** resources to use in care homes and communities

£10
a month

Helps us to support churches running the **Parenting for Faith** course and stand alongside parents

£5
a month

Helps us to support **Messy Church** volunteers and resource and grow the wider network

£20
a month

Helps us to resource **Anna Chaplaincy** and improve spiritual care for older people

 ## How to become a Friend of BRF

Set up a Direct Debit donation at **brf.org.uk/donate** or find out how to set up a Standing Order at **brf.org.uk/friends**

Contact the fundraising team

Email: **giving@brf.org.uk**
Tel: +44 (0)1235 462305
Post: Fundraising team, BRF, 15 The Chambers,
              Vineyard, Abingdon OX14 3FE

Good to know

If you have any questions, or if you want to change your regular donation or stop giving in the future, do get in touch.

Registered with

FUNDRAISING
REGULATOR

SHARING OUR VISION – MAKING A ONE-OFF GIFT

I would like to make a donation to support BRF.
Please use my gift for:

☐ Where it is most needed ☐ Anna Chaplaincy ☐ Living Faith

☐ Messy Church ☐ Parenting for Faith

Title	First name/initials	Surname
Address		
		Postcode
Email		
Telephone		
Signature		Date

Our ministry is only possible because of the generous support of individuals, churches, trusts and gifts in wills.

giftaid it You can add an extra 25p to every £1 you give.

Please treat as Gift Aid donations all qualifying gifts of money made

☐ today, ☐ in the past four years, ☐ and in the future.

I am a UK taxpayer and understand that if I pay less Income Tax and/or Capital Gains Tax in the current tax year than the amount of Gift Aid claimed on all my donations, it is my responsibility to pay any difference.

☐ My donation does not qualify for Gift Aid.

Please notify BRF if you want to cancel this Gift Aid declaration, change your name or home address, or no longer pay sufficient tax on your income and/or capital gains.

Please complete other side of form ➡

SHARING OUR VISION – MAKING A ONE-OFF GIFT

Please accept my gift of:

☐ £2 ☐ £5 ☐ £10 ☐ £20 Other £ [＿＿＿＿]

by (*delete as appropriate*):

☐ Cheque/Charity Voucher payable to 'BRF'

☐ MasterCard/Visa/Debit card/Charity card

Name on card

Card no. [ ][ ][ ][ ] [ ][ ][ ][ ] [ ][ ][ ][ ] [ ][ ][ ][ ]

Expires end [M][M] [Y][Y] Security code* [ ][ ][ ]

*Last 3 digits on the reverse of the card
ESSENTIAL IN ORDER TO PROCESS
YOUR PAYMENT

Signature | Date

☐ I would like to leave a gift to BRF in my will.
Please send me further information.

For help or advice regarding making a gift, please contact
our fundraising team +44 (0)1865 462305

Your privacy

We will use your personal data to process this transaction.
From time to time we may send you information about
the work of BRF that we think may be of interest to you.
Our privacy policy is available at **brf.org.uk/privacy**.
Please contact us if you wish to discuss your mailing
preferences.

Registered with

↻ Please complete other side of form

Please return this form to 'Freepost BRF'
No other address information or stamp is needed

The Bible Reading Fellowship is a Registered Charity (233280)

GL0221

Overleaf… Guidelines forthcoming issue | Author profile |
Recommended reading | Order and subscription forms

Guidelines forthcoming issue

HELEN PAYNTER

As this issue of *Guidelines* goes to press, I am receiving and editing the contributions for the next one. Once again, I'll be offering you a varied and lively set of readings.

If you enjoyed Pauline Hoggarth's notes on Ezra from this issue, you'll be pleased to know that she'll be bringing a set on Nehemiah next time. I'm delighted that Steve Motyer will be continuing his studies in Mark's gospel, bringing it to its wonderful conclusion. And I'm sure you'll be excited to read Stephen Finamore's second instalment on Revelation.

I'm also delighted that we'll be able to bring you a helpful fortnight on Daniel, courtesy of Bill Goodman, and Walter Moberly will be writing on Isaiah 40—55.

We have some themed readings, too, with a week on interfaith engagement from new writer Richard Martin, and one on vulnerable children in the Bible from Tim Davy. Add in some Advent readings from Jenny Hellyer and David Spriggs, and I hope you'll agree that our next issue looks set to be a challenging, stimulating and faith-enhancing edition. See you next time!

What the Bible means to me: Philip Grasham

Why does the Bible matter to me? The quick answer is because, within its pages, I get to know God – Father, Son and Holy Spirit – and also myself.

As a college lecturer, it is all too easy for me to handle the Bible as a handbook or textbook. I love the fact that I can teach the Bible and see people deepen their grasp on the Lord's greatness and goodness. Those lightbulb moments are truly precious. Yet I must always remind myself that it is when I approach the scriptures in prayer, for revelation and transformation, that the text lives and breathes. I am then reminded that I need to both learn and apply what God discloses about himself and his heart for his world.

It is the Bible that shows me who God is and how to engage with him. As history is described and explained, I discover the unchanging King of the universe. I read one cohesive account about the Lord's character and actions and both of those shine a light on his majesty and love. It is within that context that I approach my Father and my friend to listen to his voice.

In the Bible's stories, poetry and songs, there is an opportunity to encounter the most creative and imaginative being – the one who is full of grace and truth. These profound stories keep me coming back for more and more. If the Bible was written in definitions and bullet points, it would not hold the same sense of wonder as reading about David stepping forward to face a 'giant' problem or Jesus' disciples distributing bread and fish to an astonished crowd.

And, if this was not enough, I also come to find out about myself. This is not always the most comfortable aspect of biblical learning. As I read about real people portrayed in disturbingly honest and straightforward bluntness, my own flaws and faults become more obvious. Yet so does God's acceptance of me, alongside his encouragement to change. The stories of Abraham, Ruth, Gideon and Mary Magdalene invite me to both trust my Saviour and allow him to work in and through me.

I have had the privilege of teaching theology and biblical studies both in the UK and overseas. I am reminded that, while it is not always straightforward to handle or comprehend the Bible, the text itself is not dependent on years of formal study before it can be understood. As the Holy Spirit gives wisdom and illumination, there is equality for all who believe in Jesus whatever their background, status or achievements. I well remember sitting in a small mud hut in East Africa with a young man as he explained what the biblical passage that we had just read together meant to him. There were numerous insightful truths in his observations, including cultural factors which I had completely missed.

Simply put, the Bible is a precious gift, which is always in dialogue with us.

An extract from *A Christian Guide to Environmental Issues*

Environmental sustainability is a major issue for us all. In this extensively updated edition, Martin and Margot Hodson consider eight key environmental issues: biodiversity; climate change; water; population and consumption; energy; soil; food; and environment and development. Through ethical reflections, Bible studies on a different biblical doctrine for each chapter and eco-tips to enable a practical response, they outline the biblical basis for care of the environment and help the reader integrate environmental thinking and Christian faith.

The following is an edited extract taken from the final chapter of the book, entitled 'A covenant for hope'.

The People's Climate March 2014

On 20 and 21 September 2014 a coalition of organisations arranged climate change marches around the world just before world leaders were due to meet to discuss the issue at the United Nations in New York. The New York meeting was itself a step along the way to the COP21 meeting in Paris in December 2015, at which a global agreement on cutting carbon emissions was due to be signed. Preparations were made for six months before the People's Climate March. In the week beforehand the then general secretary of the UN, Ban Ki-moon, announced that he would be on the New York march, and he was joined by Christiana Figueres, executive secretary of the UN Framework Convention on Climate Change (UNFCCC), Al Gore, former vice-president of the USA, and the actor Leonardo DiCaprio. In London, The Climate Coalition organised the biggest of several marches in the UK, and those present included the actress Emma Thompson, the singer Peter Gabriel and Richard Chartres, the bishop of London, who gave a powerful speech at the rally.

In September 2014 we were on our sabbatical trip in the Sierra Nevada, Spain. We decided to make every effort to go on a march. We checked on the web, expecting that the nearest march would involve a bus journey into Granada, but we had a surprise when we discovered a march in Portugos, a village just a short walk down the road from Pitres where we were staying. We rather expected that the numbers would be small, and set off on the Sunday wondering what we would find. When we got to Portugos it was not easy to find the march, and we did quite a lot of marching just to do so! But eventually we found a brave group of environmentalists bearing two posters saying 'Si el clima es muy fragil tambien tu $' ('If the climate is very fragile, so are your dollars'). There were 13 of us and four dogs, so not quite on the scale of New York or London. We took photos of our march outside the town hall and then went to a bar afterwards for a drink and a chat.

There were thought to be 600,000 people on the marches worldwide, but did they have any impact? We are not sure, but they are a sign of hope. Two days later at the Climate Summit in New York, US President Barack Obama at least acknowledged the marches: 'So the climate is changing faster than our efforts to address it. The alarm bells keep ringing. Our citizens keep marching. We cannot pretend we do not hear them.'

Climate strikes

Obama was right and the citizens have kept marching. But it was probably not the ones he expected.

I (Martin) use Twitter quite a lot. For me it is not something I play with but a useful research tool. If you follow the right people and organisations it is possible to find out a lot of useful information, sometimes a long way ahead of the crowd. Back in autumn 2018, I spotted something unusual. A young Swedish girl called Greta Thunberg seemed to be gathering quite a following with her weekly strikes, 'Friday for the future'.

Greta started her strikes outside the Swedish parliament building on 20 August 2018. They soon grew to an international youth movement. I first saw a small strike of school children in Oxford in January 2019, and throughout that year there was a phenomenal growth in the movement. Greta became a celebrity and was invited to speak all over the world. She took two daring trans-Atlantic trips on yachts from Europe to the United States and back. Throughout 2019 and early 2020 there was a huge amount of activity. Greta's speeches were turned into a book. In January 2019, at the World Economic Forum in Davos, she ended her speech with:

Adults keep saying, 'We owe it to young people to give them hope.' But I don't want your hope. I don't want you to be hopeful. I want you to panic. I want you to feel the fear I feel every day, and then I want you to act. I want you to act as you would in a crisis. I want you to act as if our house is on fire. Because it is.

We know what Greta means, and we desperately want people to take action; there is a false hope that leads to complacency. But there is a place for real hope, not thrust on to young people, but to keep each of us going in what can be very disheartening times. And there is a place for Christian hope. In this final chapter we will look at some projects that inspire hope, and at what the Bible has to say about hope

To order a copy of this book, please use the order form on page 151 or visit brfonline.org.uk.

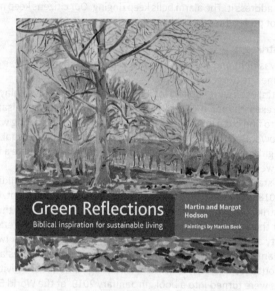

Green Reflections
Biblical inspiration for sustainable living

Martin and Margot Hodson

Paintings by Martin Beek

How should we look after the world we inhabit? Martin and Margot
Hodson bring together scientific and theological wisdom to offer
62 reflections inspired by passages from the Bible in a thoughtful
exploration that encourages both reflection and response. Themes
include 'The Wisdom of Trees', 'Landscapes of Promise' and 'Sharing
Resources'. With original artwork by Martin Beek.

Green Reflections
Reflecting on our environment with faith
Martin and Margot Hodson

978 1 80039 068 3 £8.99
brfonline.org.uk

To order

Online: brfonline.org.uk
Telephone: +44 (0)1865 319700
Mon–Fri 9.30–17.00

Delivery times within the UK are
normally 15 working days. Prices are
correct at the time of going to press
but may change without prior notice.

Title	Price	Qty	Total
A Christian Guide to Environmental Issues	£9.99		
Green Reflections	£8.99		
The Contemplative Struggle	£8.99		
The Space Between	£9.99		

POSTAGE AND PACKING CHARGES			
Order value	UK	Europe	Rest of world
Under £7.00	£2.00		
£7.00–£29.99	£3.00	Available on request	Available on request
£30.00 and over	FREE		

Total value of books	
Donation*	
Postage and packing	
Total for this order	

* Please complete and return the
Gift Aid declaration on page 143.

Please complete in BLOCK CAPITALS

Title _____ First name/initials _____ Surname _____

Address _____

_____ Postcode _____

Acc. No. _____ Telephone _____

Email _____

Method of payment

❑ Cheque (made payable to BRF) ❑ MasterCard / Visa

Card no. ▢▢▢▢ ▢▢▢▢ ▢▢▢▢ ▢▢▢▢ ▢▢▢▢ ▢▢▢▢

Expires end ▢▢ / ▢▢   Security code* ▢▢▢   Last 3 digits on the reverse of the card

Signature* _____ Date _____ /_____ /_____
*ESSENTIAL IN ORDER TO PROCESS YOUR ORDER

Please return this form to:

BRF, 15 The Chambers, Vineyard, Abingdon OX14 3FE | enquiries@brf.org.uk
To read our terms and find out about cancelling your order, please visit **brfonline.org.uk/terms**.

The Bible Reading Fellowship (BRF) is a Registered Charity (233280)

BRF needs you!

If you're one of our regular *Guidelines* readers, you will know all about the benefits and blessings of regular Bible study and the value of serious daily notes to guide, inform and challenge you.

Here are some recent comments from *Guidelines* readers:

'… very thoughtful and spiritually helpful. [These notes] are speaking to the church as it is today, and therefore to Christians like us who live in today's world.'

'You have assembled an amazingly diverse group of people and their contributions are most certainly thoughtful.'

If you have similarly positive things to say about *Guidelines*, would you be willing to share your experience with others? Could you ask for a brief slot during church notices or write a short piece for your church magazine or website? Do you belong to groups, formal or informal, academic or professional, where you could share your experience of using *Guidelines* and encourage others to try them?

It doesn't need to be complicated: just answering these three questions in what you say or write will get your message across:

- How do *Guidelines* Bible study notes help you grow in knowledge and faith?
- Where, when and how do you use them?
- What would you say to people who haven't yet tried them?

We can supply further information if you need it and would love to hear about it if you do give a talk or write an article.

For more information:
- Email **enquiries@brf.org.uk**
- Telephone BRF on +44 (0)1865 319700 Mon–Fri 9.30–17.00
- Write to us at BRF, 15 The Chambers, Vineyard, Abingdon OX14 3FE

Enabling all ages to grow in faith

At BRF, we long for people of all ages to grow in faith and understanding of the Bible. That's what all our work as a charity is about.

- Our **Living Faith** range of resources helps Christians go deeper in their understanding of scripture, in prayer and in their walk with God. Our conferences and events bring people together to share this journey. Our Holy Habits resources help whole congregations grow together as disciples of Jesus, living out and sharing their faith.

- We also want to make it easier for local churches to engage effectively in ministry and mission – by helping them bring new families into a growing relationship with God through **Messy Church** or by supporting churches as they nurture the spiritual life of older people through **Anna Chaplaincy**.

- Our **Parenting for Faith** team coaches parents and others to raise God-connected children and teens, and enables churches to fully support them.

Do you share our vision?

Though a significant proportion of BRF's funding is generated through our charitable activities, we are dependent on the generous support of individuals, churches and charitable trusts.

If you share our vision, would you help us to enable even more people of all ages to grow in faith? Your prayers and financial support are vital for the work that we do. You could:

- Support BRF's ministry with a regular donation;
- Support us with a one-off gift;
- Consider leaving a gift to BRF in your will (see page 154);
- Encourage your church to support BRF as part of your church's giving to home mission – perhaps focusing on a specific ministry or programme;
- Most important of all, support BRF with your prayers.

Donate at **brf.org.uk/donate** or use the form on pages 143–44.

God at work in the ordinary every day, from one generation to the next...

Hear, O Israel: The Lord our God, the Lord is one... These commandments that I give you today are to be on your hearts. Impress them on your children. Talk about them when you sit at home and when you walk along the road, when you lie down and when you get up.

DEUTERONOMY 6:4–7 (NIV, abridged)

Two things strike me here. First, there is the plurality to the commands given. It is not 'Hear, O parents' or 'Hear, O children's workers' but 'Hear, O Israel'. Today, parents are primarily responsible for raising their children in the faith, but the whole community has a part to play. The children of the church are 'our' children.

Second, there is a beauty to *how* we are to impress God's commands on the next generation. We are to talk when at home, when away, when we get up and when we lie down. Our task, whether or not we have our own children, is to live out our faith and let 'our' children see in our daily lives.

Parenting for Faith

Through Parenting for Faith, BRF works to resource and empower parents, carers, and churches in raising children in the faith. We strive to support as many as we can and give what we offer freely.

This is only possible because of generous donations from donors, churches, charitable trusts, and gifts in wills.

We would love your support. You can find out more about Parenting for Faith at **brf.org.uk/parentingforfaith**. If you can support this ministry financially, please consider whether you could give a regular gift. You can find out how to give regularly via **brf.org.uk/friends** or get in touch with us on **01235 462305** or via **giving@brf.org.uk**.

Your prayers, as ever, are hugely appreciated.

> Pray. Give. Get involved.
> **brf.org.uk**

GUIDELINES SUBSCRIPTION RATES

Please note our new subscription rates, current until 30 April 2022:

Individual subscriptions
covering 3 issues for under 5 copies, payable in advance
(including postage & packing):

	UK	Europe	Rest of world
Guidelines 1-year subscription	£18.00	£25.95	£29.85
Guidelines 3-year subscription (9 issues)	£52.65	N/A	N/A

Group subscriptions
covering 3 issues for 5 copies or more, sent to one UK address (post free):

Guidelines 1-year subscription	£14.25 per set of 3 issues p.a.

Please note that the annual billing period for group subscriptions runs from
1 May to 30 April.

Overseas group subscription rates
Available on request. Please email **enquiries@brf.org.uk**.

Copies may also be obtained from Christian bookshops:

Guidelines	£4.75 per copy

All our Bible reading notes can be ordered online
by visiting **brfonline.org.uk/subscriptions**

GUIDELINES

Guidelines is also available as
an app for Android, iPhone and iPad
brfonline.org.uk/apps

GUIDELINES INDIVIDUAL SUBSCRIPTION FORM

All our Bible reading notes can be ordered online by visiting
brfonline.org.uk/subscriptions

☐ I would like to take out a subscription:

Title _____ First name/initials _____ Surname _____

Address _____

_____ Postcode _____

Telephone _____ Email _____

Please send *Guidelines* beginning with the September 2021 / January 2022 /
May 2022 issue (*delete as appropriate*):

(*please tick box*)

	UK	Europe	Rest of world
Guidelines 1-year subscription	☐ £18.00	☐ £25.95	☐ £29.85
Guidelines 3-year subscription	☐ £52.65	N/A	N/A

Optional donation to support the work of BRF £ _____

Total enclosed £ _____ (cheques should be made payable to 'BRF')

Please complete and return the Gift Aid declaration on page 143 to make your
donation even more valuable to us.

Please charge my MasterCard / Visa ☐ Debit card ☐ with £ _____

Card no. ☐☐☐☐ ☐☐☐☐ ☐☐☐☐ ☐☐☐☐

Expires end ☐☐ ☐☐   Security code* ☐☐☐   Last 3 digits on the reverse of the card

Signature* _____ Date _____/_____/_____

*ESSENTIAL IN ORDER TO PROCESS YOUR PAYMENT

To set up a Direct Debit, please also complete the Direct Debit instruction
on page 159 and return it to BRF with this form.

Please return this form to:
BRF, 15 The Chambers, Vineyard, Abingdon OX14 3FE

To read our terms and find out about cancelling your order, please visit **brfonline.org.uk/terms**

The Bible Reading Fellowship (BRF) is a Registered Charity (233280)

GL0221

GUIDELINES GIFT SUBSCRIPTION FORM

☐ I would like to give a gift subscription (please provide both names and addresses):

Title .... First name/initials .... Surname ....

Address ....

.... Postcode ....

Telephone .... Email ....

Gift subscription name ....

Gift subscription address ....

.... Postcode ....

Gift message (20 words max. or include your own gift card):

....

....

Please send *Guidelines* beginning with the September 2021 / January 2022 / May 2022 issue *(delete as appropriate)*:

(please tick box)	UK	Europe	Rest of world
Guidelines 1-year subscription	☐ £18.00	☐ £25.95	☐ £29.85
Guidelines 3-year subscription	☐ £52.65	N/A	N/A

Optional donation to support the work of BRF £ ....

Total enclosed £ .... (cheques should be made payable to 'BRF')

Please complete and return the Gift Aid declaration on page 143 to make your donation even more valuable to us.

Please charge my MasterCard / Visa ☐ Debit card ☐ with £ ....

Card no. ☐☐☐☐ ☐☐☐☐ ☐☐☐☐ ☐☐☐☐

Expires end ☐☐ ☐☐ Security code* ☐☐☐ Last 3 digits on the reverse of the card

Signature* .... Date ..../......../........

*ESSENTIAL IN ORDER TO PROCESS YOUR PAYMENT

To set up a Direct Debit, please also complete the Direct Debit instruction on page 159 and return it to BRF with this form.

Please return this form to:
BRF, 15 The Chambers, Vineyard, Abingdon OX14 3FE

To read our terms and find out about cancelling your order, please **visit brfonline.org.uk/terms**.
The Bible Reading Fellowship (BRF) is a Registered Charity (233280)

DIRECT DEBIT PAYMENT

You can pay for your annual subscription to our Bible reading notes using Direct Debit. You need only give your bank details once, and the payment is made automatically every year until you cancel it. If you would like to pay by Direct Debit, please use the form opposite, entering your BRF account number under 'Reference number'.

You are fully covered by the Direct Debit Guarantee:

The Direct Debit Guarantee

- This Guarantee is offered by all banks and building societies that accept instructions to pay Direct Debits.
- If there are any changes to the amount, date or frequency of your Direct Debit, The Bible Reading Fellowship will notify you 10 working days in advance of your account being debited or as otherwise agreed. If you request The Bible Reading Fellowship to collect a payment, confirmation of the amount and date will be given to you at the time of the request.
- If an error is made in the payment of your Direct Debit, by The Bible Reading Fellowship or your bank or building society, you are entitled to a full and immediate refund of the amount paid from your bank or building society.
- If you receive a refund you are not entitled to, you must pay it back when The Bible Reading Fellowship asks you to.
- You can cancel a Direct Debit at any time by simply contacting your bank or building society. Written confirmation may be required. Please also notify us.

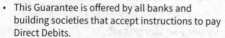

The Bible Reading Fellowship

Instruction to your bank or building society to pay by Direct Debit

Please fill in the whole form using a ballpoint pen and return it to:
BRF, 15 The Chambers, Vineyard, Abingdon OX14 3FE

Service User Number: | 5 | 5 | 8 | 2 | 2 | 9 |

Name and full postal address of your bank or building society

To: The Manager	Bank/Building Society
Address	
	Postcode

Name(s) of account holder(s)

Branch sort code

| | | – | | | – | | |

Bank/Building Society account number

| | | | | | | | | |

Reference number

| | | | | | | | |

Instruction to your Bank/Building Society
Please pay The Bible Reading Fellowship Direct Debits from the account detailed in this instruction, subject to the safeguards assured by the Direct Debit Guarantee. I understand that this instruction may remain with The Bible Reading Fellowship and, if so, details will be passed electronically to my bank/building society.

Signature(s)

Banks and Building Societies may not accept Direct Debit instructions for some types of account.

Enabling all ages to grow in faith

Anna Chaplaincy
Living Faith
Messy Church
Parenting for Faith

The Bible Reading Fellowship (BRF) is a Christian charity that resources individuals and churches. Our vision is to enable people of all ages to grow in faith and understanding of the Bible and to see more people equipped to exercise their gifts in leadership and ministry.

To find out more about our ministries, visit

brf.org.uk